The Seventh Child

The Seventh Child

Agnes Hewitt

Published by Tablo

TABLE OF CONTENTS

ACKNOWLEDGEMENTS

1. I acknowledge Aven Ross, a retired professional editor who aggressively edited my manuscript for book aesthetics compilation, as well as editing my pictures.

2. Mary Hewson who edited for grammar and punctuation and wording.

3. Bonnie McNab for allowing me to use one of the pictures from her collection for my book cover.

4. Rose Mary Goodson for the use of her collection of the evolution of washing machines.

5. Jon Neher and the Regina Public Library for helping to digitize my script.

6. Kali McDonald Final editing and preparation for publishing

DEDICATION

*I dedicate these - my memories - to my deceased Little Sister
Lydia Marie Buhr-Friesen*

And to

Her children: Jayne Bethan and James Bryan

And to

Our Mother: Tina Braun-Buhr

"

Life is a journey, sometimes long and sometimes perilous, though hopefully joyful and interesting. But it is a journey where we don't know where we are going to end up or in many cases, where we are likely to pass. Our Spanish speaking friends say before a journey, "VIA CON DIOS" or "GO WITH GOD".

- Extract from "Senior Living")

INTRODUCTION

To my surviving siblings, nieces and nephews, children and grandchildren,
their spouses and potential spouses:

Many ideas of my writings have been taken from the book, **HOW TO WRITE YOUR LIFE STORY** by KAREN ULRICH. In fact, many statements in my introduction are direct quotes from her book: **THE COMPLETE GUIDE TO CREATING A PERSONAL MEMOIR.**

"Writing memoirs is a journey with multi purposes. One purpose is to celebrate family." Namely, siblings, as this writing will take me only from my birth to the doorstep of my marriage to Dr. Hewitt. Another purpose is looking to heal past wounds and to forgive one self for bad decisions.

"Also, I wish this to serve as my children's memory of me," since I rarely talked a lot about my childhood or our growing up years. These are my memories. They may not correlate with those of my siblings. They may not all be facts as they recall them, but they are my memories on looking back on my life. Some are facts my Mother and Sister Dorothy told me at one time or another, some facts were shared by my brothers, some were gleaned vicariously by hearing adults talk. but mostly I wrote from memories from as early as age two years. If some feelings are ruffled by stating, my memories just consider they are childhood memories of incidents which happened a long time ago.

The INNER CHILD THERAPY session which I attended brought things to mind which happened years ago as though they happened yesterday, like movies. That all twelve of us siblings survived to adulthood in spite of dire living conditions is of itself amazing. I want my children to realize under what severe circumstances we were raised and how much I strived to make their lives better when they were growing up.

Another purpose of this book is to confirm the mysterious calamity of the Great Depression and how my side of the family survived. The whole world was steeped into poverty after WWII but ours was more pronounced because there were so many children in our family, although large families were common among Mennonites. Most families fared better than ours mostly because of Dad's poor work habits, such as starting to put in the crop when other farmers around were done.

Also, the purpose of this writing is to show how our parents caused the disintegration of the Mennonite culture in our family mostly because for years they did not attend services. This was due in part because distances to church services were too far to travel by horses, especially in winter times. Also in part because each parent came from a different Mennonite denominational upbringing which they seemingly never resolved.

To my knowledge there are 15 denominations within the Mennonite culture, which was started by Menno Simons, a Catholic priest who left Catholicism during the European Reformation. At that time, he had to flee for his life and wherever people harbored him he made converts, teaching SALVATION BY GRACE THROUGH FAITH, his new conviction. His followers were called Mennonites after the priest's first name.

Depending on which community my parents were domiciled we either attended a Mennonite Community Church with no denominational walls or we weekly walked one mile to an interfaith Sunday School where we were taught salvation by grace through faith.

Our Dad did read German Bible stories to us when we had to sit on the floor and listen to stories which we barely understood since we spoke a Dutch/German dialect or Pleut -Deutch at home. I believe he became discouraged and gave it up because of our inattentiveness. To me the stories he read about Abraham, Isaac, and Jacob are still my favorite Bible stories.

Dad hailed from Old Colony Mennonites and attended German Parochial School in Gretna, Manitoba where he didn't learn a word of English but he did learn to sign his name. This denomination was intent on preserving the German language although it was not really their mother tongue since they basically hailed from the Netherlands, Menno Simon's starting point, and all spoke a colloquial Dutch/ German or Pleut Deutch language.

Our mother hailed from Bergthaler Mennonites. She and her siblings all attended public school and were well versed in the English language. My mother and her sisters (my aunts), never wore anything different in dress other than those seen in the Eaton's catalogue or in pattern stores. My generation also did not wear weird clothes as was the custom in some Mennonite denominations. Mother taught us to pray, have faith, and to believe in salvation by grave through faith.

Mother liked to sing and whistle all day long while she did housework. She would pinch money from shipping cream checks in order to buy a gramophone (the kind we had to crank) and records for us to use. She taught us all to love music. I remember whenever a new record arrived at our house, we would all squat on the floor and write down words of each song. When we thought we had captured them all by comparing with each other, we would belt them out Wilf Carter style. One day mother said to me, "If I couldn't sing, I could never get through these hard times." She sang a variety of German and English hymns but also some classics like "The Lorelei" which she sang in German. I also remember my siblings and I sitting in a circle of chairs and taking turns each calling out our favorite hymn numbers out of a hymn book we all had copies of. Later my brothers bought guitars and learned to play and sing along.

My parents were both born in Canada, as were three of four grandparents – which should make us third generation Canadians. My grandmother, Anna Braun was sixteen years old when she came to Canada and was too old to attend school in Manitoba but she studied alongside with her brother and became an avid self-taught reader.

Because we weren't anchored in any particular church my siblings and I each joined the church that our spouses adhered to, which is the reason there are many faiths represented in our family: Baptist, Alliance, United, Catholic, Mennonites, Full Gospel, and Pentecostal We all had to learn to be tolerant of each other's faith. Possibly all believe in salvation by grave through faith.

Because my parents moved so often, we became exposed to different cultures: French, German, Ukrainian, and Anglo-Saxon. The word MENNONITE became almost foreign to us because we seldom lived amongst them and forget much about their culture. I later read two history books on Mennonites: IN SEARCH OF UTOPIA and VO HIN VO HARE MENNONITEN (TO WHERE FROM WHERE MENNONITES). Otherwise I would have not understood what we were supposed to represent.

Basically, Mennonites are pacifists and immigrated from country to country whenever the drums of war came on the horizon. After leaving the Netherlands, Prussia, Germany, and Poland they arrived in the Ukraine where a kind czar allotted a large tract of land to the emigrant Mennonites and allowed them to live there without ever having to go to war. They lived in the Ukraine in peace for several decades until the czar died, and a different czar came to the throne. He feared the Mennonites might take up arms and become treasonable and ordered them off the lands. Hence began a great immigration of Mennonites to Canada and the United States. My great grandparents must have come across with the first group of immigrants during the 1800 s since three out of four of our grandparents were born in Canada. My great-grandparents' country of birth is recorded as the Ukraine but not because they were of Russian descent. Their roots were in the Netherlands.

As soon as we became members of different churches, I deemed we confiscated being Mennonites. In my opinion, I gave up being Mennonite when I became a member of the Carlyle United Church after marriage. Sure, I still have Mennonite roots, but I was no longer a true-blue Mennonite. Likewise, with the other siblings who joined non-Mennonite churches.

My future husband, Dr. Wilbert Harold Hewitt, also often talked about growing up under similar dire circumstances during wartimes and the worldwide Great Depression. We both remembered how the wood fires would go out at night and how the water in the wash basins would be frozen solid by morning. Later a bagful of coals might arrive and a few coals in each wood burning stove would keep the fire smoldering overnight. But these were an expense which was not always affordable. Imagine getting up and getting dressed when the house was that cold! But my father-in-law whom I never knew, Norman Hewitt, was a hunter and fisherman. Thus, he supplied his family with meat to eat which we did not always have.

I trust that all my children, grandchildren, nieces and nephews, siblings, and whoever else may chance to read my memories will value the historical background and appreciate their parents for helping to pay their educational expenses which I did not have. Enjoy the reading!

Agnes Neta Buhr-Hewitt

CHAPTER 1: PLUM COULEE, MANITOBA

IN YOUR JOURNEY OF LIFE, YOU SHOULD LEAVE AT LEAST ONE CHAPTER.

This is your Life, your very own life. Get to know your soul. Dance your dance, sing your song, take charge of your story, Love your day. Let your heavy stuff go, embrace your blessings. Stand in your power, forgive your mistakes, forgive your enemies. Drain your secrets of their poison, heal your pain, rest your body, share your talents, practice your passions, find your bliss. Live your Life, love your Life, because the best years of your life will happen as soon as you open your hands to your happiness."

- The Mustard Seed Express

Before I formed you in the womb, I knew you; before you came to birth, I consecrated you"

- Jeremiah 1:5

THE BEGINNING

MY UNHERALDED BIRTH

I was the seventh child born to my parents, Tina and Peter Buhr. I was born in a farmhouse at Plum Coulee, Manitoba in Canada.

It was an early Monday morning on July 8th, 1930 when I decided to enter this world during the height of the Great Depression. I must have been trying to warn my parents the day before that I was about to have my coming out party because my dad had taken my six older siblings to the neighbours for the night. I imagine that my Dad went reluctantly and unhurriedly with horse and buggy to fetch the doctor at four o'clock in the morning. But neither he nor the doctor arrived on time because I decided, "this is it!" even though my mother was alone in the house.

There was no one there to pat me on the back and make sure my lungs were clear but apparently, I screamed voluntarily, and my mother wept bitterly as she had done throughout her pregnancy with me as, as she confided in me many years later. "One more mouth to feed! One more child to care for!"

"But what a blessing you turned out to be," she also told me years later. Don't worry, I was kept very humble by my siblings. My self-esteem was always at low ebb. I certainly was not a planned child, but I was a survivor, without the proverbial slap on the back, without someone to encourage my mother by saying, "Mrs. Buhr, you have a lovely daughter." No frills or niceties to welcome me into this world! The doctor must have done his thing when he eventually arrived; cut the umbilical cord and attended to my mother and possibly to me. Someone must have wrapped a little blanket around me and set me to nursing.

Before long, my dad had to fetch my siblings from the neighbours. My nine-year-old sister, Dorothy, was smitten with disbelief, as she told me years later. She ran all the way home, panting, "Is it true? Is it true? Do I really have a little sister?" Between her and me she had welcomed four brothers, plus she had one brother older than herself. She had wished for a little sister for a long, long time. Finally, here I was to fulfill her dreams and hopes.

Next began the parade of onlookers from my siblings. Dorothy had already enveloped and adopted me. After all, I was the answer to her prayers. A sister for a change, for her to dress and care for. Then the oldest, Bill: going-on-eleven with somewhat ruddy hair. Just another baby in the house but a girl for a change. Then, eight-year-old John: lean and lanky as he remained all his life, more curious than impressed. Then, five-year-old Ed with his soft, sensitive eyes – probably thinking he would never, ever hurt her. Gentle protector he always remained. Then, three-year old Paul: already somewhat rough and tumble, hoping I would be tough – yes, tough I would become. Ben: only fifteen months old, almost still a baby himself, barely walking and feeding himself. Ben and I were to become close playmates throughout our childhood years.

My poor, poor mother. She had three children in diapers (Paul, Ben, and me) and only six diapers between us to share. Each had to be washed – stat! – the minute messed and hung up to dry beside the pot-bellied wood heater. Where were the Central Relief Committees at the time to lighten mother's load with a dozen diapers at least? Unheard of it seemed. There were no Pampers. Cloth diapers were the order of the day and washable over and over again from baby to baby. But the bright spot in her life was the tiny one, the little girl who was trained ahead of her brothers. I was quick and clever and walked early, so I was told by Mother.

I have few memories of Plum Coulee but my Aunt Agnes, Mother's sister, sent me a picture of the house where I and probably all six older siblings were born, stating that she and Uncle Henry Penner and their family had lived in that same house for thirteen years after my parents vacated it. I asked my Aunt Agnes if there had been a creek with a footbridge nearby. She said, "yes there was." I vaguely remember we were all told never to walk on that footbridge, but I defied that order and crossed it one day. I also remember a very severe spanking for having disobeyed. Many years later as an adult I understood that order was for our protection in case we would fall in and drown, being too far from the house for any cries to be heard. It blows my mind that I can remember to this day some things that happened when I was age two. I also remember mother telling me that I had a girl cousin born to Aunt Annie Siemens the next day. It was still born. Sadly, they had three sons and wanted a daughter so badly. Mother knew that through the years her sister often looked at me thinking, "that's the age and size our little girl would be by now." She was sure my Aunt Annie favored me in comparison to other cousins, wishfully thinking how unfair life is. They were wealthy and could have afforded to give me so much when there were seven children in my mother's life. Why did her sister's daughter live and their little daughter died? She must have lived with that question for the rest of her life.

My maternal grandparents were Johann and Anna Braun. My mother's grandfather's name was Schwartz. A German interpretation of the word "schwartz" means black. It seems mother used to joke about her name, stating in German, "I come from the Black Brauns. What isn't black is brown." True to form, my Mother's hair was black, and her eyes were brown. Oh, that I might have inherited her coloring! I always considered her beautiful.

My paternal grandparents were Peter and Aganetha Buhr. It is obvious whom I was named after excepting my name was broken up into two names: Agnes Neta Buhr. My birth certificate says only Neta, but I have been called Agnes since starting school, so all government papers have me down as Agnes. I had many aunts and uncles on both sides of the fence. There were many cousins on both sides of the fence, some of whose names I really don't remember and possibly never knew.

In the end, Brother Bennie and I became the middle children when the complete toll of twelve children was tallied. Middle children are typically independent as no one seems to have time to care for them, so they self-care at an early age..

When I drove solo to Plum Coulee, Manitoba to attend my uncle Jack Penner's funeral I had asked my aunt Agnes over the phone if she could point me to the house where I was born, after the funeral. She did but it was only a sport where the house had once stood. When their son took over the farm the house was torn down and a new ranch-style house now stands in a different corner of the farm.

She pointed out the now deep ravine where the footbridge had once crossed over the creek. I shivered at the depth of the ravine.

My 6 Older Siblings

From left to right
Back-row: Dorothy, Ed, Bill, John
Front row: Paul, Baby Ben

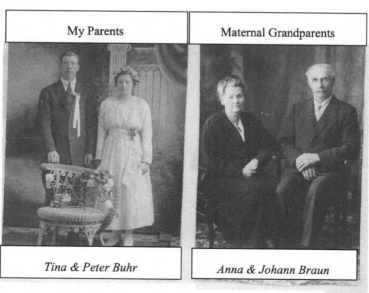

My Parents

Tina & Peter Buhr

Maternal Grandparents

Anna & Johann Braun

Grandpa Johann Braun

Grandparent's 25th Anniversary

Paternal Grandparents, Uncles & Aunts

Back: *Aunts Katherine, Maria, Helena*

Front: *Aunt Sarah, Grandma Aganetha Buhr, Uncle Erdman on lap, Peter (my father), Grandpa Peter Buhr, Uncle Henry, Aunt Aganetha (in front)*

Maternal Uncles & Aunts – Uncle Corny & Aunt Hilda's 25th Anniversary

Aunts Gertrude Schellenberg, Annie Siemans, Anne Brown, Uncles Geroge Brown, Corny Braun, Aunt Hilda Braun, Uncle Walter Groening, Aunt Lydia Groening, Aunt Agnes & Uncle Henry Penner, Uncle Jack Penner

Braun Family Reunion (what a crowd)

Cousins

Back Row: *Agnes Buhr, Ruth Brown, Ethel Schellenberg, Esther Schellenberg, Alice Schellenberg*
Front Row: *Kathleen Buhr, Judy Penner, Leona Schellenberg, Alvina Braun*

Cousins & Dolls
Agnes (back row, second from left)
Kathleen (second row, first from left)

The House Where I Was Born at Plum Coullee, Manitoba

The children in the picture are probably our cousins,
Judy and Lloyd Penner

The house at Hochstadt with add-ons, Agnes age 12.

Brother John in front of the bunkhouse Hochstadt

Aunt Annie Siemens & Family

Grandmother Braun and her stamp

OUR GRANDMOTHER BRAUN

My grandmother, at age ninety during my last visit with her, told me all about the Tudor Wars, the Wars of the Roses, and the great European Reformation. She named kings and czars. She knew their birthdates and the year of their deaths. Her historical knowledge and memory were awesome to me. On her ninetieth birthday she had named all her children, their spouses, their wedding dates, their birthdays, their children's birthdays, their children's spouses, their spouses' birthdays, her great-grand- children and their birthdays, their spouses' birthdays and named all of their wedding dates. How awesome!

Grandma Anna Braun came to Canada when she was sixteen years old. Although she did not attend school in Canada, she learned alongside her brother doing homework and became self-educated. She became an avid reader. I suspect she may have had a fair amount of schooling in the Ukraine before coming to Canada. Suffering from insomnia for many years, she would read until four in the mornings. She amazingly remembered what she read! My grandpa would get up and tell their daughters to let my grandmother sleep and they should do the work. What a dear, sweet man he was! But he was also a fighter whenever the need presented itself and his policy was always to fight for the underdog. This is a history in itself.

CHAPTER II: STE. ELIZABETH, MANITOBA

LIFE IS LIKE A HOT DOG. IT IS LONG AND FULL OF THINGS YOU DON'T EXPECT.

"My roots are grounded in the past.
Who I am is who I want to be. I'm a SURVIVOR."

(REBA'S THEME SONG)

My parent's like nomads, pulled up stakes and moved often in my lifetime. My Dad seemed to have a restless spirit and for reasons unknown he would uproot us all. The first move was from Plum Coulee, a predominantly Mennonite district, to Ste. Elizabeth, a French-Canadian district, in 1932. I must have been two years old at the time. This is where I would look out the window mornings watching my brothers walk to school when I was a little older.

I recall a lot about Ste. Elizabeth where I believe my family lived for about five years. I remember missing my brother Ben or Bennie as he was often called. He started attending school one year ahead of me and I couldn't wait till it was my turn. I remember how proudly I walked that mile south to the Ste. Elizabeth School at age six to start my Grade One. I remember walking with John, Ed, Paul, and Ben. John wasn't always there. Ed was always the referee whenever Paul and Ben got into skirmishes.

Dorothy was nine years older than me so must have turned fourteen and had to stay home to learn to work, which was Dad's rule. And learn to work she did by helping mother with the small children, the cooking, baking, laundry, cleaning, and so on. She was almost like a second mother to us. In Manitoba it was law that children must go to school until age fourteen, when hopefully they would have finished Grade Eight. Some of my siblings did not finish Grade Eight by age fourteen,

PLAY

Growing up with my brothers was an endless round of play and curiosity. Benny and I became friends for life. We played together endlessly without fighting or squabbling over toys, which were few to begin with. As we got older we made up our own games. Some days we would pretend that we were blind and we would spend all day closing our eyes tightly, groping around furniture and warning each other not to get burned by the potbellied wood heater, on which I had scorched my hands several times without any sympathies. Years later when I had eye surgery, the nurses were amazed at how well I managed with patches on both eyes. Ah, those childhood games had trained me well.

There was the Eaton's catalogue with its many dolls to cut out. As soon as we were able to hold little scissors (and sometimes we snuck Mother's good sewing scissors) we had piles of paper dolls. Sometimes we were able to find little boxes, like shoe boxes, and we would line them with furniture cut out from the catalogue. These homes had many paper dolls of children and few adults. What we lacked in real toys we made up in imagination.

Our Dad had a knack for cutting out paper horses out of a sheet of paper. He would fold it accordion pleated style, cut the outline of one horse and VOILA, he would unfold the paper and give us half a dozen white paper horses. These came in handy for taking sick kids to the doctor or to go visiting neighbors. Of course, then we needed another box for a sleigh or wagon. Oh, our imaginations knew no bounds.

MY LITTLE SISTER KATHLEEN

I was two- and one-half years old when my little sister came along. I remember someone picking me up and showing me something lying in bed beside my mother. She was the cutest, most adorable child or animal I had ever seen. From the moment I laid eyes on her I absolutely adored her. I could not wait until I was allowed to hold her. As soon as she was able to sit up. I played with her endlessly. I would find little pieces of material left over from mother's sewing scraps and drape them around her shoulders or little pieces of lace to put on her head. My little Kathleen .–She looked like a little china doll to me. Who needed dolls when you had the real thing to play with?

How I loved to comb her hair, her beautiful, dark, wavy hair. But alas, my little sister was prone to cry easily and did not seem to have a high pain ceiling – not tough and tumble as the boys had trained me to be. I seemed to have had a passion for combing her hair. As I recall, it was almost a daily ritual for me to set her down and insist that I must comb her hair. Sometimes I barely touched her hair with the brush or comb when she would cry very loudly and out of nowhere would come my Dad's thick leather strap. The question, "What happened?" was never heard. She cried, I was next to her, so I must have willfully hurt her.

I loved her way too much to ever intentionally harm her. But the charade went on for a few years. One time I had said to her, "I'm going to comb your hair. This time, don't cry the minute it hurts a little bit."

"No, I won't." But the minute my brush touched her hair she screamed. "You promised you wouldn't cry this time." "You said if it hurts a LITTLE bit."   Of course, the big, black strap followed.

Another time I was playing choo-choo train with Kathleen. She sat on a small wooden chair and I pushed the chair going "CHOO-CHOO!" She giggled and laughed until the chair tipped. It caught on a splinter in the wood floor. She couldn't have fallen hard from the low tipped chair but she howled. The lashing was particularly harsh, yet both parents sat there watching the whole procedure. They also both noted the black and blue welts on my body when I was getting ready for bed. I was told to be good from now on and the spankings wouldn't happen. What did I do that was bad? The physical smarting from the black and blue welts was not as hard to bear as the lashings given when I was totally innocent of ever intentionally hurting my little sister.

I must have been almost five years old at this time when I did the math in my head "My little sister knows by now that all she needs to do is make a little squack and I will get lashed. Well it isn't going to happen anymore." I determined from that day forward I would no longer play with Kathleen but I would go outside and play with my brothers. I felt safe with them. I knew they would never cause me to get lashings and I didn't snitch on them either if they should play rough with me or do something they were not supposed to do. I was never mean to my sister nor did I ever hurt her. I just would not play with her any more

This made Mother very sad. One day she said to me, "I was so happy that you had a little sister to play with instead of another brother. Why won't you play with her anymore?" I did not answer for fear it might result in another lashing. Mother would have understood but my Dad might consider it an affront. Didn't she remember my black and blue welts from the last time I had played with her?.

THE INNER CHILD

Many years later I took part in a therapy session called **The Inner Child.** The therapist gave me a huge teddy bear, the size of a four-year-old child, to hold and instructed me to close my eyes and pretend that this was me when I was a little child. "Go back," she said, "and remember something that hurt you very deeply. Go back. Go back. Go back," she kept saying.

Suddenly I remembered the whole scene, almost as if it were happening yesterday, like a movie. I cried. She said, "Who hurt you?" I said, "My little sister." After a discussion she said, "You should have told your parents why you stopped playing with your little sister." "And risk getting another lashing?" I asked. Mother would have understood but she would not have been able to change anything. I was wise for

my years and knew that for a fact. I had heard her chiding Dad that his\
punishments were too harsh but it only made matters worse. My Dad
might have considered it an affront, and I didn't want another lashing.

Mother once told me that she had hemorrhaged severely whenever
both Ed and Kathleen were born and for some strange reason they
became favored by Dad. Ed had stated the he cannot remember ever
being lashed by Dad. Nor can I recall ever seeing Kathleen being
spanked as I witnessed Ben and Paul often being beaten mercilessly with
tears of sympathy in my eyes. As children this favoritism was difficult to
understand.

"You must write letters to each of your parents and tell them why
you stopped playing with your little sister." "They're both dead and
gone."

"Write to them anyways." It was meant to be a therapeutic exercise
for me, I knew. I found those letters recently.

THE BARN

FUN AND GAMES

The boys had many fun games. Horse and Buggy was a good one. Two of us were elected to be horses. Benny and I were the favorites. Long strings were tied to our wrists taken back by two drivers. So, we were told to giddiup or whoa at the sole discretion of the drivers, Paul and Ed.

Sometimes we were urged to run real fast as though we were off to a fire, other times just a canter. Of course, there was no real buggy hitched to us but pretending was lots of fun and the drivers had to follow at the same speed as the horses to keep up so they geared our speed to suit themselves, fast or slow.

Another excitement the boys indulged in but were not supposed to was climbing the barn roof. There was a tall ladder leaning against the north side of the barn which was not visible from the house. Whenever Dad took off to town or somewhere, the boys would take to the ladder. It was high and must have had twenty rungs or more. Up they went, first daring Paul, then Ben and I followed. Ed always managed to follow me because he was protective and wanted to be sure to catch me if I should fall.

At the top of the barn roof, wow-wee, what a panoramic sight. You could see the whole farmyard. The pigs and sheep and calves looked like little miniatures down below. It was a sight to behold and never ceased to boggle and amaze my little mind no matter how often I was up there. The house we all lived in looked like a doll house. Walking around on the barn roof was a big challenge for me but the boys did it, so I copied, but it was very steep as I recall. Going back down the ladder was another feat. Again, Paul and Ben, then Ed ahead of me, making sure I would make it down okay and always ready to catch me if ever I should fall, but that never, ever happened. I was sure-footed and determined. If the boys could do it, I could do it.

Another pastime was fence-jumping. Cattle were kept in pastures with barbed-wire fences. When it came time to bring in cattle at milking times, the boys sometimes took shortcuts by jumping fences instead of opening and going through gates. Of course, with their longer legs and pants they could scale the three rows of barbed wires quite easily. I was getting a little older now, probably close to seven. Slacks for girls had not been invented yet. We wore dresses sewn by our mother, prim and proper every day – perhaps the same dress was worn for several days or a week. It might have even started looking grubby, but dresses were worn on a daily basis. I was still following the boys around and tried to scale fences although I had shorter legs and was wearing a dress. "Rrrip!" went my dress as it caught on a barbed hook, ripping my front wide open, exposing panties and limbs. I held my skirt together and quickly ran into the house and grabbed three safety pins and pinned the dress together. I was a sight to behold and I had to wear it like that for several days because I did not have another dress to change into readily available and my mother didn't have time to sit down and mend. I stopped playing with my brothers because I was too embarrassed to be seen outdoors.

In wintertime we would have fun sliding downhill in grocery boxes because there was no such a thing as money for fancy sleds. We had fun in any case; lots of fun. There was so much joking and teasing amongst my brothers that laughter sustained us through the poverty and the dark shadow that hung over our household. *"'Laughter helps the brain. You don't need a doctor to tell you that a giggle session is good for the soul, but new research shows that it can also be good for the brain. A recent study of people with diabetes found that laughter could reduce age-related memory loss." (www.the-open-mind.com)*

There are a few things that stand out in my memory about things that happened during that first year of my school attendance. I had developed astigmatism on my left eye and needed glasses. I could not clearly see writing on the blackboard, although eventually the teacher placed me in the front seat. My parents did not receive relief as many people did during the depression. It was considered that my Dad was a big, strong man and should be able to earn enough money to support his family. How the powers that be made this deduction I'll never know, when there were no crops and grass, or hay turned brown before fed to cattle and pigs. He was a farmer with no training to do anything else and a large family. Have a heart for his children at least!

We survived without any government aid, although we did not always have the right kind of nutrition. In wintertime when cows stopped giving milk and the hens stopped laying eggs, our honey pail school lunches consisted of lard spread between two slices of homemade bread for each of us. We never complained because this was our normal, although the horrible porridge without milk or sugar put grimaces on my face. Mother's huge gardens and her canning sealers full of fruits and vegetables all summer helped us to survive. Her endless sewing for our clothing needs kept us girls in nice looking dresses.

One day Mother presented me with glasses. "Take good care of them and always remember where you put them," became an order and a challenge from that moment on. With so many little pairs of hands around who considered my glasses a novelty, taking good care of my glasses became a daily chore for a six-year old. I'll never know where they got the money from to pay for my glasses.

Another memory of my Grade One was of a fellow named Ken Jorgensen, who was as tall as my brother John. He would often pick me up and carry me on his shoulder. That made me feel like a living rag doll. Because I was used to having brothers around and my brother John was always beside him, I did not fear this procedure although I was a very shy child.

I also remembered that we all started attending school without knowing a word of English. Pleut- Deutsch or a low German/Dutch dialect was the language spoken at home. Mother had attended public school and spoke, wrote, and read English well. With her help and the help of older siblings we picked up English quickly. By the end of Grade One we could each read our Primer or Reader fluently and print or fill in the blanks of our workbooks and speak English quite well. After a while, I remember mother started to speak more English to us at home.

Another memory I have of Ste. Elizabeth was hearing Mother scold about a lady teacher who would sniff around my brothers every school morning and scoff that they smelled of the barn. I remember mother washing all their clothes every night, including their underwear, and hanging them around the pot-bellied wood heater so they would dry by morning, hoping the teacher would stop this charade but to no avail. The sniffing and scoffing continued. Of course, the boys had to do chores in the barn after donning the clean clothes and before going to school. One day mother had enough. She wrote a letter to the lady teacher and told her in no uncertain terms that if she did not stop this procedure, Mother would send a complaint to the school board about this situation. She sent it with my brothers to deliver to her. Suffice it to say, the sniffing and scoffing stopped. This must have happened the year before I started attending school because I did not have a lady teacher in

Grade One. My first teacher was Mr. Pokrant, teaching Grades One to Eight in a one-room school.

I remember that we lived in a two-story house at Ste. Elizabeth. There was a living room downstairs with a door to the outside on the south wall where the boys would bring in armfuls of wood. Also, on the south wall were a chesterfield and a window. Next to the window pushed into the corner was a dresser made of brown wood with a large mirror. In front of the dresser stood Dad's large beige leather covered rocking chair, which I used as a stepladder to climb up and sit on the dresser to comb my hair and seemingly admire myself. Coming down the step ladder chair was not too reliable, as it would rock, and I would fall between dresser and chair many times during ages three and four. Some people never learn.

In front of the big chair in the center of the room stood the pot-bellied wood heater which heated the entire living room. In the north-west corner of the living room stood a large double bed where mother and the smaller children slept, which included me for a few years. In the north-east corner of that room stood a single bed where Dad slept. In the middle of that wall was a doorway into the kitchen which had a window on the north wall and one on the east wall. On the north-east wall stood quite a large dining table with chairs surrounding it. In the north-west corner of the room stood a large wood-burning kitchen stove. On the west wall beside the stove was a doorway to the outside foyer. Beside the east window was a stairwell going to the upstairs bedrooms which were underneath the gables and didn't allow for much head space when adults were standing up. There was a window on the east wall at the top of the stairs. Sister Dorothy had the first bedroom which I shared with her in time, possibly by the time I was around four years old.

The older boys slept in the other bedroom. I believe there was another window on the west end of the gable. I also remember that Dorothy liked to read in bed till quite late by coal oil lamp and sometimes got scolded for it. She was nine years older than me and she remained my mentor for the rest of my young life, possibly because of the bonding when she rejoiced in having a little sister and in sharing a bedroom at this time. I don't remember ever wearing pajamas. We wore slips and panties Mother made out of Red Rose flour bags. These were worn all day under dresses and she also sewed nightgowns out of flour bags, I think.

I also remember that below the stairwell was a cellar where potatoes, vegetables and canned sealers were kept, and at times the trap door was left open by mistake. I remember a few tumbles from the top of the stairwell all the way down in the cellar. I was always too brave to cry.

I have come to the conclusion that the only way parents can raise a large family is if the older children take responsibility for the younger ones and become responsible for helping with laundry, cooking, and other duties. I remember that big sister Dorothy was like a second mother to us young ones and was able to help Mother with much of the work. She must have reached the age of fourteen before I started school and was mother's helper and learning to do all housework. That was dad's policy.

BABY ABE

Abe was four months and four years younger than me. He was born while we lived at Ste, Elizabeth but in a Winnipeg hospital. He was the first of Mother's babies to be born in a hospital but so were all succeeding ones. I always thought Abe was such a beautiful sibling. He had blue eyes and blond hair. When I was a little older I thought Abe should have been a girl. I would put Kathleen's dresses on him and would clip his hair back. He never cried when I combed his hair. Abe was a very docile sibling, quiet and well behaved. Over time he came to be the kindest, most generous brother who would give his shirt to anyone who needed it.

NEIGHBOURS

I really don't remember names of any neighbours at Ste. Elizabeth. I do remember mom, dad, myself possibly four years old, and I don't remember who else of my siblings went to visit neighbours with travelling mode of a big sleigh and a team of horses in mid-winter. I remember that there were little girls my age at this house. I also remember coming home with a tiny little toy car. When mother found it in my coat pocket there was a severe spanking and Dad had to hitch up the horses to return it. Hopefully he could have multi-tasked and swung by the store for groceries.

CHAPTER III: HOCHSTADT, MANITOBA

"A house is more than paint and wood. When we move away, we leave behind the memories of who we were then. Life is not a dress rehearsal. We get it one time only."

I don't think we lived at Ste. Elizabeth for more than five years because I started Grade Two at the Hochstadt School after my parents had moved again, this time to the Hochstadt School District. Hochstadt, Manitoba was not a town but a district. It was predominantly a German speaking district with some Lutherans, high German speaking neighbours, and some Mennonite families who spoke low German or Pleut- Deutch..There were some Anglo-Saxons and a few French speaking neighbors. There was a family by the name of Koop who ran a family grocery convenience store sort of connected to their home. The closest town was Grunthal, about fourteen miles away from our farm where my parents did most of their grocery shopping or where Dad went for farm supplies during seedtime or harvest.

Lydia, David, Abe, Kathleen, Ben, Paul, Ed, and I all attended school here from time to time as they reached the age of six. until they were age fourteen. I don't remember John attending school here He must have turned fourteen years of age before we were living at Hochstadt. Lydia's attendance is dubious to me, but David says he and Lydia started Grade One together and David is definitely in the pictures. You will always notice him wearing a tie.

I remember taking Grades Two to Eight at Hochstadt School. Mr. George K. Reimer was our teacher for Grades One to Eight for most of the years that we attended that school. He taught Health and Religion to all classes combined.

We lived between two school districts, Hochstadt and Gravelridge. Gravelridge School was about one and one eighth mile from where we lived, and Hochstadt School was about that much less than a mile. So, our family was appointed to attend Hochstadt School. We walked barefoot to school until October. Many of the neighbours' children did the same.

In the Gravelridge schoolhouse some organization held talent nights on Sunday evenings. A certain man, whose name I don't remember, had choir practice during the week at this school. He taught by rote instead by note. 1, 1,4,3 and so on. On Sunday evenings he had us, his choir, sing at talent night. Sometimes there was a Christian speaker there. One speaker told my Dad that he could tell which ones of us young people were his children and if he knew the age and rank of each child he could tell him what each of us were like. Birth-order and sibling dynamics was a university study that interested me in later life.

I was very spiritually inclined at that point of my twelve-year old life and I would lie awake for hours fearing that not all my siblings might be ready at this second coming. Occasionally there would be travelling ministers speaking in the Hochstadt School always speaking in German. Because we were now of school age and German was taught in our school, we could understand the speakers. The messages were always the same. Salvation by grace through faith and the second coming of the Lord is near. Be ready!

Although I was thirteen going on fourteen, I chummed with eighteen-year-old Nettie Dyck. She and her older brother would drive to choir practice, sometimes picking me up while on my way walking and definitely taking me home if they were there. There were two older teenage, seventeen -year-old boys, both named Pete - Pete Gunther and Pete Schellenberg – who would also catch a ride with them. One of them slid into the back seat with me one night and started groping me. I forgot we were not alone in the car and told him where to go in loud, no uncertain terms. "Stop that! Leave me alone." Everyone in the front seat roared with laughter. It became a joke that I was teased with for the rest of our stay at Hochstadt. Some of these boys came to choir practice merely to see which girls they could escort home, either on foot or by car if they could catch a ride. Later, sometimes one or the other of the Pete's would walk me home or part ways home.

Nancy Koop, an eighteen-year-old Evangelical Christian started an inter-faith Sunday School in the Hochstadt School on Sunday afternoons. We were never told that we must go but on Sundays we would don our best clothes – the newest dress mother had sewn for me – and off we'd walk one mile to the same schoolhouse we had walked to all week.

We learned so much. She taught Old and New Testament Bible stories, and the life of Christ. We memorized the Beatitudes, the books of the Bible, and many verses. She taught us many hymns and choruses which are still being sung in many churches today. Best of all, she taught us salvation by grace through faith and how to accept Jesus as our personal Savior, a teaching that stayed with us through life and to those who have proceeded us to their deathbeds. She also encouraged us to memorize 300 Bible verses in exchange for a free week at the Canadian Sunday School Mission Camp at Gemili, Manitoba. I did this and attended this free camp and became totally inundated with spirituality and Biblical teachings. The next year I did a correspondence course on the book of John and earned a second week of free camp. Here I won a Bible for having the best notebook in the camp.

I remember when we first arrived at Hochstadt we had moved into a one room shack. There was a large double bed in the north-east corner where Mother and we smaller children slept. In the north-west corner stood the wood-burning kitchen stove. In the south-west corner was Dad's single bed. There was a couch on the south wall where Dorothy slept. On the east side was the outside doorway. I think a tall chest of drawers was placed between the large bed and only door in and out of the shack. The floor was dirt and I believe we might easily have been termed as "dirt poor".

What happened to the big beige leather covered rocker? I never saw it again. What happened to the dresser with mirror? I think there was a little bunkhouse where the older boys slept. What happened to the big house with more bedrooms?

In time Dad built a loft with a ladder where we school children slept. I think we slept on blankets or quilts and covered ourselves with more blankets or quilts. We had never heard of air mattresses at that time. In time a wooden floor was laid, and a large kitchen was added with a wooden floor, which Dorothy later painted dark brown with pastel sponge patterns. There was a pantry built in with shelves to hold dishes, pot and pans, and groceries. A large kitchen table with benches and chairs surrounding it on the south wall where windows were located. An outside door with an inside screen door was hung on the north-east end which included a little foyer.. A lot of traffic was ushered in and out of that doorway. In the middle of the north wall was a doorway into that little old shack room which doubled up for living room and bedroom. There was never any basement or cellar, so the pantry had to hold everything. In time a large bedroom was added, large enough to hold three or four beds with mattresses. The original shack also became enlarged and the outside became covered with siding, which was later painted maroon, as were all the other add-ons. Finally, we had a fairly decent looking house and a little warmer than originally. A window on the east wall now replaced the original doorway as a small porch was added with the entrance and screen doorways.

BABY DAVID

Mother brought home another baby boy from the Steinbach Hospital, Baby David, born on June 30th, 1937 at 6 a.m. He must have arrived soon after we moved since he is seven years younger than I am and I turned seven that July. My help was needed that summer indoors. A lot was expected from me at age seven. One of my jobs as dictated by sister Dorothy was to fold laundry and such: a pile of laundry; baby diapers, toddlers' clothes, tea towels, towels, pillowcases, and so on. At this stage there were three pre-school aged children in our house hold; Kathleen age five, Abe age three, and little Baby David. I know we all took turns pushing David in the baby carriage, feeding him his bottle and pablum. He was a happy child in his carriage as he remained all his life; always cheerful in spite of grim circumstances. When David was six years old, he had rheumatic fever. He missed attending school for one year, then started Grade One at age seven along with little Lydia who arrived one year after he did. He attended school until fourteen and completed Grade Seven. Kathleen says she read to David by the hour when he was sick. The rheumatic fever affected his heart which took his life following open heart surgery in later life. I will always remember how cheerfully he kept saying, "I'll make the surgery. Don't worry," and he did, but he dropped dead a few years later.

NEIGHBORS

Some neighbors I remember at Hochstadt were a family of Sawatzkys. They had a family of young people. Some names that come to mind are George, Katherine (who was my age), Pete, Abe, and Anne. We were back and forth visiting with them a lot. Katherine was a true and loyal friend. Another family that lived close by were Hieberts. We played lots of games in the evenings with neighbours' kids. Friesens, Funks, and Millers were more neighbours we socialized with.

PIG KILLING TIME

Among Mennonite neighbours pig killing was a community event. We were allowed to stay home from school and help. Neighbouring men and women worked diligently at every aspect of the butchering and of getting the meat sliced and shredded for sausages. I remember helping to clean out the pig's intestines. Water was poured through the narrow and wider intestines until totally clean inside and out. Then they were dredged in salt inside and out. When one of the adults declared they were now totally clean, the salt was rinsed off and they were slipped onto a grinder where someone else was pushing meat to be ground into the very clean intestines for sausages. I remember being helpful in this area. For a few months we enjoyed having meat for meals but there were no refrigerators at the time in our house. Meat was sometimes packed tightly in cardboard boxes and set outside to freeze with constant vigilance that dogs would not find the cache.

THE WAR YEARS: 1939-1945

Germany declared war by their leader or "fuhrer", Adolph Hitler. He wrote a book called *Mein Kamph* meaning "My Battle", in which he declared that he was going to conquer the world.

My parents were farming in a German settlement and German grammar was on our school curriculum. We had German Primers or Readers which we learned to read plus some grammar was being taught. When I was in Grade Four, teachers in Manitoba were no longer allowed to teach German because the war was against Germany and because of the atrocities that were executed by that country.

Mennonites were pacifists and the church fathers traveled to Ottawa to obtain amnesty for Mennonite young men to become conscientious objectors and would not be conscripted to go to war. Instead they would need to do volunteer work. Brother Bill was assigned to work on farms, but brother John was sent to a mine. Here he was terrified and soon reasoned that going to war could not be any more frightening than working in the dangerous, scary, dark mine. So, he enlisted voluntarily as did his cousin, Pete Friesen. Pete's Dad and my parents sat in our kitchen grieving over what their sons had done. "I didn't think I raised sons to pick up guns to go to war and kill," spoke Mr. Friesen. To make matters worse, they both brought home French Canadian Catholic wives. The bottoms fell out of the parent's lives. Catholicism yet. It was by far the greatest of all calamities. A totally misunderstood religion by the die-hard Mennonites.

The war songs came over the radio daily, on an hourly basis. We couldn't help but become inundated and sing along with them all day long till we knew them all word for word from memory. One morning, Mother became quite upset hearing me sing the popular war songs as it reminded her too much of her Johnny in the army. But the war ended in August 1945 before John had to go overseas and he came home again.

John and his wife, Rose, lived on a farm at Giroux, Manitoba where my parents had moved to by that time before the war ended.

FAWN (FLICKA)

One day our brother Ed was plowing in the field walking behind a team of horses. He noticed a doe standing and looking at him. He would walk the full length of the field and turning team and plow around to plow the field length coming back and the doe was still there unmoved. He stopped the horses and walked over towards the deer. She disappeared. He bent down and found a newborn little fawn. He patted it, then went back to plowing. The dough came back once, seemingly sniffed her baby and never returned. We think she smelled human scent on her baby and abandoned it. At the end of the day Ed picked up the little fawn and carried it home. Our mother quickly found a bottle with nipple, filled it with milk and the little fawn was bottle fed for several weeks, perhaps even for a month, then it was given its own dish and leftover food off the table, the same as our dog, Fido. There was no such a thing as store bought dog food and certainly no money to buy it with.

For some time Fido and Flicka each ate out of their own dish, but dog and deer became very friendly and eventually both ate out of the same dish at the same time. There is a picture somewhere of the two animals eating out of the same dish but I can't find it among my collection. We called the fawn Flicka after the story *"My Friend Flicka."* Fido and Flicka were at home in our house and walked in and out at will. In time we put a red ribbon around Flicka's neck. For about one year it stayed close to home. But then it started wandering off, at times staying away overnight and returning in the morning. After a while it would stay away for several days, then almost a week, but always came back. We heard a report that some travelers had seen a deer with a red ribbon around the neck on the highway. They had stopped the car and the deer walked towards them as if wanting to be friendly. It obviously had no fear of humans. One day, possibly one and a half years later, it disappeared never to return. We were sure some hunter found it an easy target during hunting season. It had become part of our household and we missed it. On retrospect, perhaps we should have turned it loose sooner and prepared it for the wilds.

We lived at Hochstadt for about seven years. I remember taking Grade Two and completing Grade Eight in that school.

Flicka

Kathleen (age 11) feeding Flicka

Lydia, David & Fido

Abe, David, Lydia, and Flicka

Front Row: Lydia, David, Abe, Kathleen.
Baack . Row: Agnes, Ben, Paul, Ed

Front Row: Lydia, David, Abe, Kathleen

BROTHER BEN

Ben liked to tease me. One of his favorite tricks was to hide behind the door whenever he saw me coming and quickly give my hair a gentle pull and sometimes not so gentle. I found this little trick somewhat annoying at times. This went on repeatedly for some time. One day as I was approaching the house, I saw a shadow flit across the screen door. So, I backed up to the well, pumped a dipper full of water, and as I walked through the screen door I turned and poured it over his head. He never tried that little trick again.

But a teaser he remained to his dying day. When we became teenagers and my friends and I would resort to the topic of boys, he would be filled with glee after my girlfriends left because he knew exactly which boys to tease me with. Soon I realized that whenever he knew my girlfriends were expected, he would hide in a closet during the entire visit, hearing every word that was said. We soon found another home to meet to share our girly secrets.

BABY LYDIA

In the meantime, another baby sibling was born. David's birthday was June 30th, 1937. He was four days less a year old when Lydia Marie was born on June 26th, 1938. Her beautiful, short life was very endearing to all of us. Kathleen and I hovered over her. Kathleen was six years old and I was eight by then. We took turns taking her for rides in her carriage and stroller. We fed her Pablum and gave her bottle feedings. When she was old enough to sit up, we would play with her. Mother made a little white dress for her when she was about one year old. She looked so sweet and angelic. She was quickly learning to walk and talk. When she was a little older, she loved to play. Often at bedtime she wasn't ready for bed but would say, "I want to play!" Lydia and David were almost like a pair of twins and played together endlessly. They both started attending school together. David had rheumatic fever when he was six years old and missed one year of school Lydia was six years old and David was seven when they started Grade One. David always maintained that learning came easy to Lydia but was challenging for him.

WASHING DAYS

Washing clothes was not as simple as turning on a few taps of water and adding laundry detergent. We had to heat water in a long, deep, tank-like tub on top of a wood heated stove. As much as possible it was rainwater caught in barrels during summertime. In wintertime, snow was melted stovetop the day before. Washdays were all-day procedures, followed by the drying outside on the clotheslines. Sometimes clothes were brought in frozen stiff and hung all over the place to finish drying indoors. We had an old washing machine which was a brown tub on legs and a long handle which had to be pushed back and forth for twenty minutes in order for the clothes to wash clean, a great improvement over the scrub board. This was the Cadillac model compared to more dated models and the washboard. I don't know who invented twenty minutes of maneuvering the handle for clothes to get clean but it seemed to have been written in stone. At that time it was deemed necessary for the water to be boiling hot in order for clothes to become washed clean. We were to take turns pushing that handle. "Agnes, you do the first ten minutes, then Kathleen the last ten minutes". Shared tasks. It was amazing how often Kathleen could develop a stomach-ache just before her ten minutes were to start. Who could blame her? It was a boring, tedious chore.

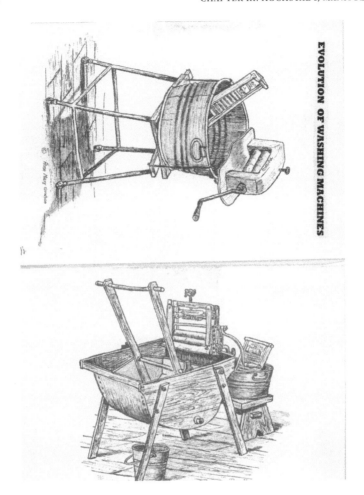

EVOLUTION OF WASHING MACHINES

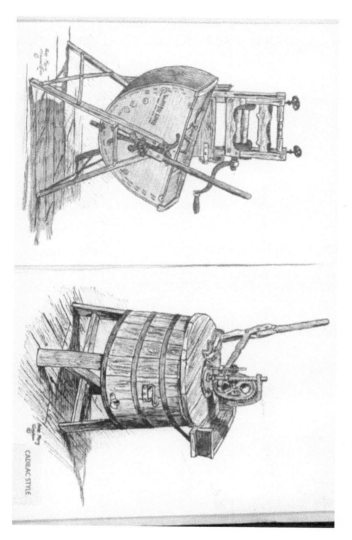

RUNNING WATER

For many years Dad hauled water from some public well. It is hard for me to imagine how many barrels had to be hauled daily for cooking, laundry, and for the barnyard animals: the horses, cows, sheep, pigs, and even fowl. One summer day a well driller drove into our yard and started drilling. He struck water and from that time on we had an ever flowing well. Mother called it an artesian well. It was controlled with a large pipe and had a huge galvanized trough built round it. The water was so cold and clear. The animals loved it too, especially on hot days. We joked about having running water, but we did the running with pails full of water from well into the house as we had no indoor plumbing.

LAMP LIGHT

Can you imagine not being able to turn on a light switch to light up a room? When we were growing up, we studied and read by lamplight. We had coal oil lamps with a wick that was lit, and a glass chimney set over the flame. If we were lucky, we had a coal oil lamp in several rooms. Cleaning the glass chimney was a job which none of us liked. We could get covered with soot from hands to elbow as we had to reach into the glass chimney to rub off the soot. In time, mantle lamps came into use. These were a great improvement with little mantle bags tied around the opening of the gas flame. These little bags were lit and exuded a bright flame when the lamp was turned on. These lamps had a handle and could be hung on a nail on the ceiling and light the entire room.

DOROTHY'S SOCIAL LIFE

Dorothy was a worker and work delegator, but she was also a socialite. She loved to play guitar, sing, and yodel Wilf Carter style. By age seventeen she went to dances seven nights a week, played her guitar, sang and yodelled till she had a hoarse throat. She would sleep in, but whenever she decided to get up everyone was put to work. She would give directions a few times and all were at their

Dorothy and Nancy Coop

posts of duty. At this stage of her life she wanted to be called Doris. Later, it reverted back to Dorothy again, so the two names became interchangeable. At age seventeen she fell in love with a young man named John Gerbrandt. He hung around our house a lot and soon became part of the family. It was quite obvious that he was in love with my sister. They went to parties and dances together. Every so often she would invite her friends to come to our house. The kitchen table and chairs were pushed tightly against the wall. My Dad would take out a small accordion and strike up dance music and soon the dancing began. We school kids were allowed to stay up and watch. After a while, John left to go back to his parents' home at Carrot River, Saskatchewan to find work for the winter months. Dorothy really pined for him. She didn't enjoy socializing as much without him.

But then something happened to Dorothy. She had a few encounters with an evangelical Christian, by the name of Nancy Koop and this young lady led her to the Lord. Dorothy immediately made a three hundred and sixty degrees turn (as my mother phrased it) and she categorized everything she used to do as EVIL. Dancing was sin. Singing and yodelling were sin, as one must only sing spiritual songs and hymns. Movies were evil. She shared her joy of salvation and was anxious for everyone in the household to be saved and to see things as she did. Christianity became so important to Dorothy. It was her wish and prayer that all her siblings would become born again Christians and to live according to her standards. She definitely had a strong influence on the spirituality of our entire family. She explained salvation to me in such a way that I understood at age eight while we were picking saskatoon berries.

We were sent to pick saskatoons, choke cherries, pinch cherries, and high bush cranberries by the galvanized tub full. My mother's survival passion for all of us was to can sealers full of fruits and jellies. Once the wild fruits were picked our job was to sort and all the stems and dross garbaged Then they were canned according to whether they were canned as fruits or jellies. She must have been able to buy bags full of sugar by paying with money from shipping cream. These sugar bags made good tea towels and dish rags.

Besides canning wild fruit, my Mother always had a huge garden, an acre or so it seemed when she sent us to hoe and weed. Kathleen and I were hoeing one morning in the garden surrounded on three sides by trees. The fourth end was so far from the end we were working we decided to remove our blouses and suntan. When the sun was high at eleven o'clock, nearing noon we suffered not from suntans but from sun burns. A few sleepless nights followed nursing our burns.

Mother canned peas, green and yellow beans, corn, beets, pickles, and anything else the garden yielded. She worked tirelessly all summer providing nourishment for all of us for the winter months ahead. In the meantime, we had our fills of lettuce, radishes, cucumbers, corn on the cob, tomatoes, melons, watermelons, and so on. In the fall pumpkins, cabbages, cauliflower, and carrots were brought in by the wheelbarrow. Besides all these vegetables, mother also had beautiful flower gardens every summer. I think she could have lived in her gardens all summer.

My mother was a praying Christian, but it had nothing to do with being Mennonite. I think she wanted to pray us all into heaven and taught that God is love, that Christianity is believing in salvation by grace through faith. As born-again Christians we want to follow in Jesus' footsteps and do what is right. She loved each one of us. One day she said to me, "We have so many children but if anyone asked me to give one of you away I could never part with any of you." It was unconditional love for each of us. Another time she said, "I have to discipline each of you in a different way. If I speak sternly to Paul, he just becomes rebellious. But if I ask him gently to please do something for me, he will willingly do anything."

Mother also had an uncanny discernment if anything was wrong in any of our lives. After harvest, my older brothers would leave home to find work, often in lumber camps. There were no phones or emails and the boys were not very swift about writing letters so usually we didn't know until they returned in spring where they had been all winter. One March Saturday morning my mother walked the kitchen floor wringing her hands. Finally, she said, "Children, I want you all to stop what you're doing and pray for your brother Bill. I don't know where he is and I don't know what he's doing, but I know he is in terrible danger." So, we all stood on the spot and prayed silently for our brother Bill. A few weeks later Bill came home. I heard mother asking him, "a few Saturdays ago about eleven o'clock in the morning, where were you and what were you doing?"

"Oh, I was in a lumber camp. My partner and I were cutting down a great big tree. When the tree began to fall, we, both ran in opposite directions hoping the tree would not fall on either of us because that means game over. The tree fell on me that morning. When I crawled from under, my partner was pale as a ghost and he said, "I didn't think I'd see you alive again." I didn't hear mother telling him that we had prayed for him exactly at that time. Perhaps he never knew that mother's prayers had saved his life that day.

WEDDING PLANS

When John Gerbrandt returned in the spring, wedding plans went full tilt ahead. He must have shared her beliefs as they enrolled in Catechism classes in the Bergthaler Mennonite Church. Later I learned that this was a requisition by this church that they must take Catechism classes and be baptized before the church would marry them. The church warned against worldliness and taught salvation by grace through faith, just as Mother taught us and we learned in Sunday School. They encouraged Bible studies and meditating and to live good sincere Christian lives.

The morning their weddings bands were announced in church, Dorothy, John, mother, and dad had gone to church and my Aunt Eva and Uncle Aaron came to visit. I seemed to be the oldest child around as the boys were probably doing chores in the barn. I went out to greet them and to invite them in. I looked at my younger siblings at play and I was totally embarrassed. Their faces and their clothes were so dirty. At age nine I took it upon myself to grab each one by the wrist and tell them they had to come in and get washed. I didn't meet with resistance as I had a vice grip on their wrists. First Kathleen: a clean dress, then I washed and dried her face and let her go. Next Abe, then David and Lydia with the same procedures. When the church goers arrived at home my Aunt Eva couldn't stop raving about what a nine-year-old girl could do. But I wasn't even given a pat on the back as Dorothy and mother just busied themselves with preparing lunch for our guests.

Dorothy turned eighteen in June and the wedding date was set for August 27th, 1939. It was obviously a very passionate love affair, gathering from their constant embracing and extended kissing sessions.

WEDDING BELLS

It was a beautiful outdoor wedding. John and Dorothy worked hard to make the yard look presentable for wedding guests. Chairs were borrowed from I-don't-know-where! Dorothy borrowed Aunt Eva's wedding gown. The weather was bright and sunny, a lovely harvest time day. The minister who baptized them also married them, a Rev. Henricks. Very soon my sister and her new husband left for Carrot River, Saskatchewan to live with his parents. How we missed her, especially my mother and me. I had to grow up right now and become mother's helper.

Outdoor Wedding

Dorothy and John Gerbrandt

LIFE WITHOUT DOROTHY

I was nine years old at the time and the indoor workload fell on my shoulders as I soon became harnessed as mother's helper. Dad always made sure the boys were kept busy in the barn. I felt duty-bound to help my mother as much as I possibly could. I knew that she had a heart condition and I lived in constant fear that she might die and what would happen to us then? It didn't alleviate my mind when our teacher, Mr. George Reimer, spent an entire health class including all grades talking about heart conditions, stating that cardiacs often die instantly without warning. Many times, I would run home the entire mile or walk so fast that my brothers often called me "aeroplane," just to check up on mother. It was always a priceless relief to see her up and about or even lying down. I pitched in the minute I came home from school and helped her with the work. I had an uncanny sense of what needed to be done and did it. Rarely did mother need to tell me to do this or do that. I always believed this was an inborn attribute and would be inherited by my children.

The winter I was twelve years old I would see mother lying down daily when I came home from school with dinner dishes still on the table and cream separator unwashed. I would heat water on the wood stove, clear the dinner dishes off the table and wash them, meanwhile heating more water and then wash the cream separator. Then I would proceed to make supper, peel potatoes, cook sausages, make gravy, set the table. After supper I would do the dishes again before I began to do homework at ten o'clock at night, Mother spent much of that winter in bed. She tried to help me with my homework. I needed to write book reports but did not have time to read books. So, mother read them and told me word for word what she had read. Then I wrote the book reports.

Every Monday I had to stay home to do the laundry. On Saturdays I did ironing and scrubbed floors, besides baking bread. I never asked why she was sick in bed but always assumed she had been ordered to rest because of her heart condition. Why wasn't I told the reason why? Nine days after my thirteenth birthday I was to learn that she had been pregnant and threatening to lose the baby who turned out to be little Henry. By that time mother was a grandmother of Dorothy's two boys, Leonard John and Ed Corny.

JOHN AND DOROTHY AND BOYS

Next summer, John and Dorothy and boys decided to move back home into our already crowded house. Just how they pushed things around to make room for themselves and their accumulated possessions and two children I can't really remember. I do remember two things: Dorothy really believed that she was more help to mother than hindrance with so much more food, cooking, laundry and work; she needed someone to babysit their children because they wanted to go visiting and I took it over.

The overcrowding and busyness all winter became stressful. It turned out Dorothy was pregnant and expecting in March. John went about building a new one-room little house in our yard where they moved into with their boys. This made more living space (lebens raum) for everyone. On March 7th, 1945 Anna Katherine Gerbrandt was born in that new little house with the help of a local mid-wife, Mrs. Harder. We enjoyed those little boys, Leonard and Edward and it became quite sensational that baby Henry had became an uncle as soon as he was born. The three little boys learned to play so well together and were more like three little brothers. It was so sweet to also have a baby girl amongst them. There were still so many children running around and playing in our yard. It was a good, happy family time.

That fall John and Dorothy decided to move back to Carrot River, Saskatchewan to live with his parents again with their three little children in tow. I don't remember what they did with their little house, but they must have sold it for removal before they left. Their leaving was always followed by a period of a deep aching in our hearts.

I don't remember what we all lived on for groceries, except much of what we ate was home-grown. I do remember we shipped cream and the cream checks had to spread over many expenses such as materials for mother to sew with, for all our clothes were home-made by mother. Our slips and panties were made with Red Rose flour bags, but many of our dresses were made with seersucker material, probably the least expensive material of the day. I can't remember whether mother made night gowns out of those flour bags, or whether we wore our slips for the night.

CAN YOU IMAGINE?

Can you imagine a time when there was no electricity or running water or furnace, which are important commodities which we didn't' have when we were growing up? The boys were often sent into the bush to chop down trees for firewood for the kitchen stove and for the pot-bellied heater in the living room to heat the rest of the house in wintertime. It was back-breaking work to chop down trees all day, but then each tree had to be cut into smaller logs. In time, a power saw was rigged up so two boys lifted a tree little by little to chop into logs. After this these logs had to be split into smaller pieces of wood again. Work on the farm was never easy.

BOYS PREPARING FIREWOOD

FIREWOOD TO HEAT THE HOUSE & FOR COOKSTOVE

Bringing Home the Firewood

OUTDOOR BACKHOUSE

I forgot to mention our "unflush" toilet system. We and all our neighbours had a little backhouse, on the inside of which there was a little bench with two nice round holes where people could sit and relieve themselves. The little building was sitting on top of a slightly trenched hole. And there was the Eaton's catalogue available for toilet paper. Some of the coloured pages were quite stiff and a little harsh on the back-side skin and needed to be crumpled and crushed before use.

If we were lucky a box of mandarin oranges might arrive around Christmastime. These wrappers made the most delightfully soft toilet papers. We had never even heard of Purex or Scotties toilet paper. This backhouse made a convenient hiding place if kids tried to get out of work. Usually the job was done by someone else in the meantime. At nighttime there were little potties under each bed to avoid having to go outside in the dead of winter nights. Where I live now in a retirement lodge, it's amusing how the elderly like to reminisce about the outhouse and types of toilet paper we didn't have.

OUR HUNDRED SHEEP

One day our Dad took a notion that he wanted to own one hundred sheep, so he drove around the countryside buying up sheep until the toll counted one hundred. It wasn't just that simple. They all had to be fed and sheared. Our brother Paul voluntarily took over the job of shearing. It took a specialized type of shears, but he was able to get them. We all stood and watched as the wool rolled off each sheep to the ground. To do this one hundred times took him a week. It was not the end of the wool either. It had to be washed and washed. The first wash was brown and dirty and smelled so bad, but it had to be washed until the water was totally clear. Then the wool all had to be dried on window screen material stretched across wooden frames. Once dried it all had to be carded, then used to make quilts. Those were the warmest quilts ever, made of pure sheep's wool.

Brother Ben and the sheep

THE HOCHSTADT SCHOOL

During the seven years that I attended the Hochstadt School, as many as six members of our family attended that school at the same time: Lydia, David, Abe, Kathleen, Ben, and myself. Notice that in every school and home picture, brother David is wearing a necktie.

The school was an anchor in our neighbourhood. All the children in school were our friends and would come to our house in the evenings to play games. There was such an age span of children in our family that there was a play mate for children of any age. "Anti-Anti Over", "What time is it Mr. Wolf", "Pom-Pom Poll Away", "Hide-And-Seek", and many other games were often played in the evenings by the older children in the neighbourhood.

Mr. George K. Reimer was our teacher for all the grades and all the subjects until he retired, when a Mr. Nick Toews became our teacher when I was in Grade Seven and Eight. Later when Nancy Koop started a Sunday School in the schoolhouse, the school became a venue for Christian education. All school-age children in our family walked the mile to Sunday School on Sunday afternoons without ever being told that we must go. That schoolhouse brings forth many memories of good old school days.

The Hochstadt school also became a venue for church meetings. Many evangelical ministers came to speak and conduct church services here. Some spoke in the English language, but others spoke in high German, often maintaining that German was after all our mother tongue when it really was not. I remember often being in attendance with my parents and probably a few other siblings.

The school yard was often the scene of community baseball games including adults and school children. The Hochstadt school was a multi-purpose community centre.

The Hochstadt School

Grades 1-8

Back row: Ben & Agnes
End of middle: Kathleen
Front row: David, Abe, & Lydia

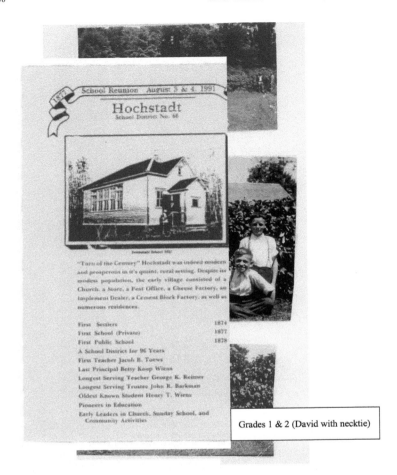

Grades 1 & 2 (David with necktie)

LITTLE BROTHER HENRY

I was just thirteen years old when mother came home from the hospital with a little baby boy, born July 17th, 1943 at Steinbach Hospital. I was so shocked to learn that Mother had another baby after she was a grandmother of two boys. Why didn't someone tell me that was why she spent those months in bed? Did they think I was a baby and didn't know anything? In my confused teenage mind, I decided to have nothing to do with this baby sibling. I was particularly angry at my Dad for making Mother have another baby at this stage of her life.

One day I was washing the cream separator after I came home from school. Inadvertently the ring flipped from my soapy hands and fell on the baby's face who was in the carriage close to me. I went to retrieve it and poor little Henry's face puckered up trying not to cry but hurting. He was so cute with curly blonde hair. I felt so sorry that I had hurt him, so I had to pick him up and comfort him. At that moment, I bonded with him and he became my special baby brother Henry. Every day after I came home from school, I had to wash his diapers and baby clothes and bathe him before making supper. My oldest brother Bill was nearly twenty-four years old when Baby Henry was born so that our mother bore children over a twenty-four-year span.

Leonard & Ed Gerbrandt & Uncle Henry

HENRY AGE 8 YRS. 1951

Leonard, Ed, Uncle Henry

Time for school

HENRY'S SCHOOLS

HENRY 1953 GRADE IV STEINBACH SCHOOL

HENRY 1956 GRADE VII STEINBACH ELMSDALE SCHOOL

a picnic

Uncle Henry & Jim

Henry, David & Abe

jamming

BETTY & HENRY

HENRY

HENRY & FRIEND

BETTY, MOM, COOKIE, BARB

HE LOVES HIS GUITARS

WHAT A GREAT LIFE

LIVING AT GIROUX

Our house at Giroux

hauling water on a stoneboat?

horse & buggy

plow horses?

MOTHER & CHILD

PLOWING FURROWS

CHAPTER IV: GIROUX

Within the garden of my heart where flowers of friendship grow, there are
blossoms of remembrance, forget-me-not so blue, and purple velvet pansies to
tell my thoughts of you…and roses that will always bloom whatever be the
weather. Whose fragrance is the memory of days we spent together.

We lived at Hochstadt for probably seven years. I started Grade Two at Hochstadt School and finished Grade Eight. When I completed Grade Eight, I wanted to go to high school. I did not receive any encouragement. My dad's philosophy was, "Girls don't need an education to wash dishes and diapers." I said, "Okay, dad." He indicated that there would be no financial help forthcoming. I didn't expect any as I knew they didn't have any to give and I did not ask for help from anyone.

It seems to me my parents must have moved us to Giroux the summer after I finished Grade Eight, after I turned fourteen. I can't remember too much about the upheaval of moving. I do remember the sale of the 160 acre farm to a local farmer, a Mr. Bagalke. The house I know was swiftly torn down and a new modern house built for their young married couple.

I remember in the new farmyard there was a small, red building with a large trough and an ever-flowing artisan well. There was a large sized red barn and seemingly the idea was to go into dairy farming by buying up twenty-four cattle and shipping milk. My brothers all seemed to be onside, willing to work hard milking cows, feeding them, cleaning barns, feeding little calves for shipping, and so on. I also remember that we had pigs and chickens and turkeys, and our mother always had a large garden.

In the house I remember a large kitchen/dining area with an outdoor entrance on the west wall. There was a small window and small foyer with multiple hooks to hang outdoor clothing beside the north side of the door. There was a larger window on the south wall and a long table with a bench and chairs surround. On the north wall of the kitchen was a doorway into the dining room. Beside the doorway in the kitchen stood the wood-burning kitchen stove where mother and I baked one dozen loaves a day and two dozen buns on Saturdays.

My brothers were now almost full-grown and conscripted to stay home and run the dairy farm. They were all good bread eaters, so we needed to do a lot of baking. This chore was mostly between mother and me. I remember a long counter where we kneaded bread dough and set them in pans to rise and bake and where we rolled the buns. There must have been kitchen cupboards on the east wall.

The next room was a dining - room and north through an arched doorway was a small living room. There were two bedrooms, one doorway from the living room and one from the dining room. Kathleen and I shared the one leading from the dining room. The other bedroom held a double bed where mother and smaller children slept and dad's single bed. The older boys all slept in a large bunkhouse.

Kathleen, Abe, David, and Lydia attended school. They had a long two-and-one-half mile walk and were seldom given rides. I do remember taking them to school with horse and buggy one day. I received permission from the school board to teach Sunday School in the schoolhouse, although mostly my younger siblings attended. I remember being very lonely here because I wasn't having school friends. I really missed my Hochstadt school friends and neighbours.

It was from here that I took my second week of free Canadian Sunday School Mission camp after completing a correspondence course on the Book of John. Mother took me to the train station in the town of Giroux, four miles from the farm, with horse and buggy. She also picked me up again with horse and buggy a week later. It was at this camp that I won a Bible for having the best kept notebook in camp, I was kept busy and worked hard to help mother but was also taking my grade nine by correspondence. I soon realized that I couldn't take all the subjects because there was too much housework for me to do, so I dropped about half of the courses hoping to take them up the next year. One of the classes I dropped was Mathematics. I never did pick them up again and so from then on, math was difficult for me when I later took Grade Ten by General Adult Education and ever after.

BROTHERS

JOHN & BILL

JOHN

ED

BROTHER BILL

BROTHER BILL & HORSES

Back Row: BEN & PAUL
Front Row: BILL, JOHN & ED

BROTHER ED & COLT

My 5 older Brothers

NEIGHBOURS

Some of our neighbours here were Gauthier, Lesperance, Grahams, Hornics, Messabroskis, and Broskis. One New Year's Day we were invited to the Messabroskis for dinner. They had quite a Ukrainian spread. Mr. Messabroski kept saying, "YEAT! YEAT! PEOPLES! DON'T SHINE!"

After having been at the Canadian Sunday School Mission Camp I was again very inundated with spirituality. I joined the Western Tract Mission and was sending tracts to a list of people sent to me, and I was sending a list of neighbours for other people to send tracts to. One day, one of my lists went to one of the neighbours by mistake. I received a letter from this neighbour that was not too cheerful,

I hardly socialized at all at Giroux, except whenever friends from Hochstadt or relatives came to visit. I remember my aunt Lydia was a visitor who told me never again to stay up all night to study for exams. She had no idea how much house work I had to do to help mother with before I could sit down to study.

Through the tract mission I had a short correspondence with someone by the name of Jake Siemens. He seemed to be like-minded about missionary work. So, in my euphoric mind I believed he was the man God had ordained for me. I fantasized and waited for the right time of meeting by God's ordainment. I turned down other would-be suitors. But Jake Siemens never came.

There was a small chapel in the Town of Giroux, four miles from our farm. A lady named Mrs. Klassen and a young man named Menno Reimer came from Steinbach to conduct services. There were other church elders who were speakers and song leaders. They seemingly heard about us living on the farm and they made it their mission to come to get us and bring us to their services. Sometimes we could persuade Dad to take us via horses, but if we didn't show they would come and get us by car. They included all my younger or older siblings, and me and my parents if we would go. Sometimes they picked us up on Sunday mornings for Sunday School. At Christmas time they would have gifts for each of us. They seemed to be determined to shower our family with love. They originated from Emmanuel Mission Church, an evangelical church in Steinbach, Manitoba about fourteen miles from Giroux.

"Who will go lord? It is I, Lord? I hear you calling in the night. I will go, Lord, if you'll guide me."

When I was fifteen years old one evening, I was all alone in the girls's darkened bedroom. I was praying and fancied I saw an outline of Jesus' face. He was calling me to go as a missionary to Africa. "How can they believe on someone if they have not heard? Who will go for me?" I decided I would go. From that moment on I was determined to train and apply to African Missions. For starters, I thought that I must take Religious Studies. This was eventually arranged by babysitting for John and Doris who later bought a house and lived in Steinbach. Doris was expecting a baby and would be needing my help. .I would be attending the Steinbach Bible Academy. and living with them. I did not start attending the Academy until my parents made yet another move.

I remember at this time I decided that I should be baptised on the confession of my faith. Mrs. Klassen was fervently encouraging me to be baptized by immersion in the Emmanuel Mission Church. I honestly don't know why I decided to go back to the Bergthaler Mennonite Church and go through a series of catechism classes conducted by Rev. Henrichs in the Steinbach branch. My Dad and Mother faithfully drove with horses the fourteen miles to Steinbach for I-don't-remember-how-many weeks of Sundays. I had to memorize catechism answers which each participant was in turn asked to answer in German. When the series was completed, we were asked to kneel in church, and we were baptized by sprinkling water "in the name of the Father and of the Son and of the Holy Spirit." We were all dressed in black. I still don't know why I made that choice. I might have been truthfully accused of being somewhat fanatical at that time of my life. I must have been sixteen going on seventeen years old.

WEDDING BELLS, AGAIN!

John and Rose were married by a civil service in Winnipeg, Manitoba on December 22nd, 1945. I believe that Pete Friesen and his wife stood up for them. The women were sisters, and both were raised Catholic, therefore Rose never believed they were legally married because they were not married in a Catholic Church.

She had a daughter named Marlene from her first husband. John and Rose had a little daughter, Betty Marie Buhr, born on September 28th, 1946. I remember being asked to help at their house while Rose was in hospital and after she came home with Baby Betty Marie. This niece is still special to me. I remember they lived in Winnipeg, Manitoba at the time and the city was quite accessible by train from Giroux and we travelled there frequently.

CANNING FACTORY AT ST. CATHERINES, ONTARIO

Life on Earth is expensive, but we get one free trip around the sun every 365 days.

I also remember leaving by train to Ontario to work in the canning factory. A train car full of girls from the west were offered to have their train fare one-way paid for by the company with the arrangement that the amount would be deducted off our first paycheques. We all stood in front of a moving assembly belt, wearing gloves to protect our hands, and we would pick up peaches as they came along the belt and cut them in half with a sharp gadget fastened at eye level so the pits fell into pails underneath the cutting knife. We were paid by the number of pails full of pits the boss lady punched on a card pinned to our backs, so the faster we could work the more we got paid. I was by far not the fastest worker and perhaps also not the very slowest.

This was a short term six or eight weeks of employment. We had to pay for our own train fare home, back to Manitoba. I did not get fabulously rich by it. I think I made a second trip to St. Catherine's, Ontario canning factory after our parents had moved to MacGregor. While there we visited the amazing Niagara Falls. We also walked across a bridge to New York. Here we visited a huge zoo with hundreds of different species of monkeys. Awesome! I made some new friends and connected with friends from Hochstadt. I also had an admirer who pursued me. Both times I left the summer/fall job early after speaking to mother who reported that she was ill.

ST. CA

MY ONTARIO FRIEN

MY ONTARIO FRIENDS

Baskets of Fruit

ONTARIO HYDRO CLOCK

(AGNES FACING FWD)

My Friend Frieda

AGNES(OH TO BE SLIM AGAIN)

Niagra Falls

TWO LITTLE LOST BOYS AND A DOG

I also vaguely remember that at some point John and Dorothy came home to live with us at Giroux. One day, little Henry (who was possibly three years old) and his nephew, Leonard (who was possibly five years old by this time) had wandered off on the road to school. They were missed around the house and yard. I went looking for them and saw a small truck driving towards me with our dog barking and jumping up at the passenger window. The driver stopped and said, "I think I have what you're looking for and that dog would not let them out of his sight." I thanked the man and walked home with two little boys and a collie in tow.

I remember they did live with us for one year. John and Dorothy did eventually buy a house in Steinbach, Manitoba and settled down. Possibly Leonard got to be of school age, and they needed their own permanent address and school district to register their upcoming school children.

I have no idea why we left Giroux because I seem to remember that things were going quite well financially with shipping milk and calves at the dairy farm. I remember that when I had mentioned that I wanted to get a job in Winnipeg which my Hochstadt friends were doing, my Dad said that if I left he would have to sell the farm, that they could not manage the farm without me. This certainly made me feel shackled. At least it was a realization that I contributed massively to the indoor work on the farm. One of my brothers said our dad was tried of cattle farming and wanted to go back to grain farming which later became his doom.

I heard a voice at evening softly say, "

Bear not thy yesterday into tomorrow; nor load this week with last week's load of sorrow. Lift all thy burdens as they come."

PICTURES ABOUT ME

AGE 14

AGE 16   Baptism

AGE 15

Age 17

age 18

age 18

FRIENDS/FAMILY

EMILY ISAAC

HELEN WIEBE

Suzy koop

JUSTINA STOEZ

SUSAN PENNER

Paul, Agnes, Rose, John

AGNES, MOTHER & ROSE

AGNES AGE 9, DOROTHY AGE 18

SUMMER ACTIVITIES

UR GROUP AT CANADIAN SUNDAY SCHOOL MISSION   **C.S.S. MISSION CAMP 1943**

DailyVacation Bible School Groups

Our Summer Team   children's tent meetings

CHAPTER V: MACGREGOR, MANITOBA

Yesterday is history. Tomorrow is a mystery. Today is a gift. That's why it's called the present.

I think we moved to MacGregor, Manitoba by my eighteenth birthday. I remember Bill coming home when mother mentioned that I had just had my eighteenth birthday. "She's eighteen and not married. Well, she's an old maid." From that moment on I was referred to as "the old maid". Dorothy had married at age eighteen so that was the role model. Girls should marry by age eighteen and become housewives and have babies, but I had other ideas. I was going to be a missionary and so needed many years of studying in front of me. My heart and soul were ever on that goal. Bill himself did not marry until almost thirty. Kathleen was not referred to as an old maid the minute she turned eighteen – it was my very own special label.

Many things happened at MacGregor; some that took a tragic toll and I find difficult to remember and to write about. Where we moved to was known as the Richardson Farm.

The house we moved into was huge. There was quite a large bedroom in the south-west corner of the house. I think there was a window on the west wall. There was a large living room with a pump organ where I later practiced my piano lessons for a short time. There were windows on the west and north side of the room. There was a huge kitchen dining area with a large table and chairs surrounding it, a pantry and a wood burning kitchen stove. Windows were on the north and south walls. A long porch where the cream separator stood as well as some other furniture, including a table where we sorted berries and shelled peas and slit beans and so on. Below floor level there was a room sized food cooler which was only a few feet deeper than ground or floor level. It was totally cemented and cool temperature. That wass where the vegetables went for the winter.

A stairwell on the north wall of the kitchen to the upstairs where there were three or four bedrooms. Kathleen and I shared a fair-sized bedroom which had a window on the east wall and a clothes closet which we shared. The boys shared the other rooms whenever they were at home. I don't quite recall the layout. There was quite a small bedroom on the north side with a window on the north wall. Another bedroom had a window on the west wall and another bedroom a window on the south wall. A white verandah wrapped around three walls on the outside of the house.

I was still kept busy with cooking and housework and a lot of laundry., helping Mother. Our washing machine was in a shed where the wringer was electric and plugged in to an electrical outlet. The washing machine was not electric but had to be worked with a long stick handle for twenty minutes. Somehow the laundry was left up to me and no one else was ever around on laundry day. This particular morning I was pushing heavy men's jeans through the wringer when my hand started to go through the wringer along with the heavy pants. I managed to turn off the wringer but by this time I also had to pull my hand back through the wringer. My hand was immediately swollen to three times its normal size and totally blue. Someone took me to the emergency at the Portage La Prairie hospital. The hand was lanced the blue blood clots squeezed out by the doctor without the freezing taking. The doctor did try to freeze, but as soon as his needle hit my skin the blood squirted out. I had to grit my teeth at which the attending nurse commented, "you took that pain in silence!" I spent a few days or weeks with a bandaged hand.

I suffered from chronic fatigue one summer. It was indescribable. To have to walk downstairs to the kitchen was almost impossible if it had not been for rails to hang on to. When I managed to get downstairs, I went straight for the chesterfield, crashed, and lay there. Mother took me to a doctor. He picked my finger and very quickly discovered the problem. "You are low on iron. These pills should fix that." A prescription of large brown pills taken for a few weeks perked me right up again.

In the fall I turned eighteen, I went away to live with John and Dorothy in Steinbach, Manitoba in exchange for baby-sitting and attended Steinbach Bible Academy. Dorothy was expecting that winter and had three small children. Almost nightly one or the other of the little children started a crescendo of crying. Dorothy was so weary of nightly having to settle first one, then each of the others till they finally fell asleep again. I slept on the couch in the kitchen and was awakened each time by the crying. They did not want me, but "MOMMY!" for whatever their needs were.

John was employed in a service garage. He was always very mechanically inclined without having any training. He was quite moody at times. I studied hard at Bible Academy and made some friends. I knew I was needed at home but Kathleen took more responsibility I was sure. I became involved with Child Evangelism and taught a weekly group of children. After a few false alarms, Dorothy went to the Steinbach Hospital and Susan Martha Gerbrandt was born on February 5th, 1949. I stayed till the end of April when Bible School year ended, and Dorothy had returned from the hospital for a few months.

Dorothy was a strong woman and always maintained she was happily married. I knew and saw that she endured much by calling on God for help in faith. I returned home for the summer months to work with garden, meals, and laundry.

The next year my cousins in Winkler, Manitoba persuaded me that in their Bible School students could take their Grade Ten or Eleven from end of April till end of June by adult education. I had to take advantage of any short cuts, so I registered with Winkler Bible School starting in January and took Grade Ten by end of June. I became very friendly with a girl by the name of Susan Penner and brought her home with me one weekend. I had free room and board in exchange for helping with housekeeping for an elderly widow in Winkler that winter. I also had a few clients I cleaned floors for weekly and earned a little money.

SISTER LYDIA'S ILLNESS

Meanwhile at home, our youngest sister Lydia, had developed kidney infection. When we first moved to MacGregor the Beaver School stood across the road from the south-west corner of our parent's farm. My siblings attended school there and didn't have very far to walk. Seemingly Lydia did not enjoy attending school as one morning after I thought all the school-aged children had left, I found Lydia hiding in a clothes closet upstairs and she was determined not to go to school that day. I had to call Mother and I'm not sure just how it was resolved.

While I was away, apparently, they had to go to school to MacGregor by school bus because of the change of farm housing location. David says they had to walk one- and one-half miles to the Number One Highway and often stand and wait for the school bus in the cold of winter. Seemingly, Lydia caught cold and infection in her kidneys and became ill with nephritis, an illness which later took her life as a young mother of two children. The doctor ordered total bed rest. She had to be carried up and downstairs from her bedroom and was told to consume lots of fruit juices. To this day, I feel guilty that I was not home to help.

I did not know that at the time Kathleen was not at home. Dad had hired her to work at John and Rose's while he took her salary not for the purpose of helping his family or his ailing daughter. Although mother phoned me at the time about Lydia's illness, she did not tell me that Kathleen was not at home to help. She should have told me.

While Dad wanted to go back to grain farming, the dust storms blew away the profits. Sunflower crops were the rage in Manitoba at that time as a huge sunflower oil factory had been built in Winnipeg and generous contracts were offered.

One hundred acres of sunflower seeds were planted besides other crops. A dust-storm blew out all the newly planted seeds. The one hundred acres had to be re-seeded. The dust blew through closed windows so that we had to sweep the dust from windowsills into dustpans with a brush.

Eventually Dad could not pay rent to the owners and I heard what must have been the lady, Mrs. Richardson ordering Dad," Get off my land!" in no uncertain terms. I don't remember how many years we lived in that big house – possibly four.

Dad then had a house moved onto one hundred and sixty acres of land where the bush had to be cleared first, which he apparently owned, so says brother Abe. Apparently, a barn and chicken coop were built with the help of older boys and perhaps some neighbours. Abe and David were left to do the chores: milk cows and feed the pigs and so on. David says Dad spent more and more nights away from home until winter- time when he did not come home at all. Bill had it figured why.

Dad would borrow money and give the cows as collateral. One by one the creditors would come and collect one cow after another.

Ed and Paul were working for the PRFA. Ben and Abe started working in Portage la Prairie, Manitoba at the time. Later Abe also got a job working for PRFA. Bill then hired David to help him with farm work for fifty dollars a month. He would give David five dollars and give forty-five dollars to mother, plus he butchered a pig and hung sausages and meat in a cold shed as reported to me by David. My poor, mother. I can't write this story without weeping. I wasn't even there to help..

MACGREGOR COMMUNITY MENNONITE CHURCH

There were quite a number of Mennonite families in the area which included Austin, Manitoba, a neighbouring town. There were Friesens, Rempels, Bauschmans, Hamms, Buhrs, Unraus, Wiebes, Leppkys, Nuesteaders, Thiessens, Sawatzkys, and more. The Hamms called a meeting and all the Mennonites agreed to have one community church instead of splintered up into several smaller groups. They were able to rent a chapel and conducted Sunday morning services, Sunday School, and Talent Night on Sunday evenings. We also had choir practices conducted by Elmer Hamm. We sang on Sunday mornings and sometimes Sunday evenings.

Elmer was very much in charge. He tried to get many visiting ministers but if none were available, he took charge of the pulpit. It was an active group. We made many friends at this place. At one time I was asked to teach Sunday School. The young people were in the "pairing off" stage and we catered to a few outdoor weddings during the next few summers. I was still focused on going to Africa and discouraged any would-be daters.

MORE WEDDING BELLS

Eva Friesen was visiting her sister, Mrs. Bauschman in MacGregor while my parents lived there. Bill was introduced to her and started dating her. When she left to go back to her parents' home in Schoenfeld, Saskatchewan they started corresponding. Bill made a few trips to visit her and her parents. Eva also returned to visit her sister a few times. Eventually Bill went to Schoenfeld, Saskatchewan and they were married in her parents' home on July 24th, 1949.

When Bill brought her home to meet his family Mother welcomed her with open arms and made her feel loved. Her sister, Mrs. Bauschman and Mother proceeded to invite people to a reception. I wasn't home at the time. I think I was somewhere teaching Vacation Bible School and couldn't get a ride home. Perhaps one of my brothers would have come to fetch me. I should have been at home to help.

Bill had a house built before they were married where they lived on their farm close to the Town of MacGregor, Manitoba.

LYDIA'S ILLNESS WORSENED

Lydia was in the Children's Hospital in Winnipeg, alone. Her condition became chronic and incurable. She needed blood transfusions every few months after that.

She would later take the bus from Steinbach, have her blood transfusion and take the bus back home. I shake my head in wonder how she managed all that at such a young age. Were John and Rose available to meet her there or to take her back to the bus? Her condition happened before dialysis was in use.

A pair of Nightingale twins from Steinbach, Manitoba were flown to New York for kidney transplants. One twin had two healthy kidneys, the other had two diseased kidneys. That was the first and only successful kidney treatment known at that time.

I remember being at John and Dorothy's when Lydia Ruth was born on April 6th, 1951 when they lived in Steinbach and my parents still lived in MacGregor. They were determined to name their baby after me but

I persuaded them not to. Then they named her after Lydia, Ruth Lydia, which made me happy.

CHAPTER VI: STEINBACH, MANITOBA

"The Way We Were
What was too painful to remember,
We simply chose to forget.
So, we remembered the laughter"
"The Way We Were" by Allen & Marilyn Bergman
History is shaped by the one who is doing the telling.
"Watch against anger; for, like drunkenness, it makes a man a beast"
William Penn

THE DARK SHADOW IN OUR HOME

There was always a dark shadow in our home. Our parents were always arguing, and our home was dark with strife. The constant bickering and angry put downs and belittlements were heard all day by all of us. I used to think that our Dad could swear at Mother for five minutes in one breath. We all felt anger at our Dad for the way he treated our Mother.

There was a history passed down that at one time he had beat her while she was pregnant. That he had been a philanderer as well was also known. Our anger towards Dad about the way he treated our Mother was deep rooted. Also, the way he beat and lashed some of us for no reason was fuel added to the fire.

The years of anger came to a head. David says Brother Bill had loaded Mother, possessions and family and moved us to Steinbach in his big red truck. I don't remember anything about the move. I remember crying buckets full of tears because of our parents split. It was true Dad was abusive and we all hated him but there was a bonding. I think it happened during the summer of 1952. Where was I?

Or did I always block the upheavals of moving from my mind? I can't remember the move from Ste. Elizabeth to Hochstadt, nor from Hochstadt to Giroux nor from Giroux to MacGregor or MacGregor to Steinbach. I never remember how we got there but now we are there. I don't remember packing my belongings or helping Mother packing or what vehicle moved us. David said Brother Bill's red truck moved us to Steinbach. We were in a rented house on Second Street, across from a church.

I remember taking my final year at Steinbach Bible Academy and graduating in 1953 after the family moved to Steinbach and I lived with Mother, together with siblings Kathleen, David, Lydia and Henry. I had also applied to Africa Inland Mission soon after my graduation from Bible Academy. They required that I have either an R.N. or a teacher's certificate because at that time it was easier to send professional people to a foreign country. That meant I must first of all get my high school credits before I could apply to Teachers' College or nurses training, so I had a long row ahead of me.

There was such a shortage of teachers in Manitoba at the time when the Department of Education offered a six weeks Summer Course for anyone interested in teaching after which they could teach on Permit for one year. I was accepted for this course along with a few other Bible School

THE HOUSE AT STEINBACH

graduates. While Mother and the younger children were living in Steinbach, I went away to Thicket Portage, Manitoba to my first permit teaching school. I remember having a ride to Winnipeg with a couple who had befriended me during Bible School, where I must have caught the train to northern Manitoba. I was crying when we left the little house and I said good-bye to Mother. and Lydia. I was homesick before I left and for a long time afterwards.

BIBLE SCHOOL

Susan Penner & Agnes Buhr

Susan Penner

Bible School trio singing in hospital

My Child EVANGELISM CLASS

MY GRADUATION FROM STEINBACH BIBLE ACADEMY

Gladwin Plett, Alvina Plett, Eveline Reimer, Agnes Buhr, Ramona Loewen, Ben Friesen

GRADUATION S.B.I. 1953

SUMMER SCHOOL FOR PERMIT TEACHERS

LINING UP FOR MEALS

Pam, Agnes,Ann,Pat,Evelina   Irene,Pat,Ann,Pam

AFRICA INLAND MISSION

CHAPTER VII: THICKET PORTAGE SCHOOL

"You raise me up so I can stand on mountains.
You raise me up to walk on stormy seas.
I am strong when I am on your shoulders.
You raise me up to more than I can be."
- Brendan Graham

MY FIRST PERMIT TEACHING SCHOOL

I arrived at the Thicket Portage School on a Monday morning. I introduced myself, then we sang "God Save the Queen" and said the Lord's Prayer. After this I went about learning the children's names and teaching Reading, Arithmetic, and other subjects. I was teaching Grades One to Four with forty children, ten of whom were definitely challenged.

The day went by without any problems. When four o'clock came I dismissed the children and told them it was time to go home. I was met with a surprise rebellion. "We don't want to go home." They ran around the outside of the school and as many times as I said, "Boys and girls, I want you to go home this minute!" the rebuke was echoed, "We don't want to go home!"

They started throwing stones at the school and I was afraid they might break windows. I opened a drawer and spied the strap. I stood on the school steps waving the strap and shouted, "Boys and girls, if you don't go home this minute, this is what you'll get!" Away they scampered like little mice. My deductions: when all else fails, use the strap. They never tried that again.

I can still see myself on my first day of teaching. I was wearing a red blouse and a black skirt and stood on the school steps waving the strap. What a lark!

My other problem: I had to share the teacherage with a committed Jehovah's Witness. She did not believe in Christmas. "The star we all sing about at Christmas was put there by the devil not by God," she said. "How do you explain that?" I asked. "It was the star that led the wise men to the king, and they told him they were looking for the Christ child to be King of the Jews. That's why so many babies were killed." She didn't believe in Sundays either. I ended up reading her catechism so that I could understand where she was coming form. But we shared meals and cleanups.

The teacherage was attached to my school which was very convenient. She taught Grades Five to Eight and had only twelve students. When the inspector came, he delegated the ten challenged children into Edith's room. Teaching was much easier for me after that.

I appealed to the children's good side and told them that I wanted them to be a well-behaved class so that when the inspector would return, I would be proud of them. I suggested that we would need rules and I wanted them to make the rules and make up the punishments if children did not behave. Their number one rule if anyone didn't behave their first punishment was to stand in the corner for two minutes. Rule number two if the same child misbehaved again, he must sit in the library for ten minutes and do extra work in Arithmetic. The third time this same child misbehaved he or she must receive three straps across the hand by the teacher.

I made big conduct charts and recorded any misconducts. Any child that had not been strapped would receive a prize at end of month. These were their rules coming from children Grades 1 to 4, most were Indigenous or Metis and a few white children. They were bound to live by these rules. One incident comes to mind. A boy in Grade Three came to me and said he had three marks on the conduct chart, and he deserved to be strapped. He held out his hand and said, "Strap me." I looked at the pathetic looking boy. He had missed a week of school due to illness and pus was running out of his ear. "I don't want to strap you,"

"Strap me. I deserve it," he said, and he stood there holding out his hand. You can believe that I tapped his hand very lightly three time.

I also had Health charts asking each morning if teeth had been brushed, knowing quite well that they could lie about it but thinking this chart made them health conscious.

I organized the Christmas concert which was expected. Some of the items, like a formation of a green pine Christmas tree, wanting all the boys dressed in green and another drill by the girls all dressed in white required costumes. I bought crepe paper and sent patterns and instruction home to mothers. I read in a senior's paper many years later that crepe paper costumers were the order of that day. Edith did help on the night of the Christmas program by directing the right groups and the right children onto the stage at the right times.

I was very homesick and worried about mother and Lydia. I was planning to go home for Christmas and not return. Of course, I had to notify the board but did so indirectly by speaking to Mr. Unrau, one of the board members. Mr. Unrau was also the pastor of an evangelical mission church, whose services I had been attending. He came over to talk to me and pointed out that if I left now, I might not stick with anything that I had committed to. In fact, he gave me a stern counselling and talking to and let me know that the school board would take a dim view of me leaving now.

So, I bought a return ticket to and from Winnipeg. From there I would take the bus to Steinbach to spend Christmas with my mother and siblings. Enroute to Winnipeg a young fellow teacher sat beside me in the train car. He had been teaching at Norway House and had to fly to James Bay, then embark on "the slowest train to China," which we were on. He opened the topic of religion by saying, "There are so many religions in the world and everyone believes their religion is the right one. But there is only one thing that matters. Two pieces of wood nailed together and the person who hung there." It was an explanation which I've used many times since to explain Christianity.

I wish I had written to mother more often. I knew she was always worrying and hoping we were alright whenever we were away from home. It was thoughtless of me not to write more often. There was always a part of me that wanted to spare her from any problems, thinking she had enough of her own. Another part of me wanted to be independent since Dad had told me not to expect one penny from him, which I did not expect to begin with.

At Thicket Portage we were surrounded by several lakes, namely Landing Lake, Paint Lake, and Wintering Lake. Also, there was a Burnt Wood River somewhere within the geography map. These bodies of water helped to climatize the forty below weather.

There was a storekeeper at Thicket Portage, Mr. Cook who offered to take us across the ice-covered lake in a bombardier to a nickel mine at Thompson Lake, Manitoba. A bombardier is like a small car only operates on skiis, therefore can go across ice. He took us to their rough shod dinning shack. What it amounted to was a long, rough building with tables nailed together with rough boards and benches to sit on of the same rough boards nailed together. They poured coffee into shabby looking mugs and the coffee was so strong a spoon could almost stand up straight in it.

These were many bunkhouses on the premises. It was unbelievable to me that little more than a decade later a large city, Thompson Lake, Manitoba became developed here and my niece Betty Marie Buhr lived there with her husband and two small children. During its boom time they had everything including Wal-Mart, Tim Hortons, Robin's Doughnuts, General Hospital (where Betty worked & trained as a nurse), and a movie theater, with a population of at least ten thousand in order for it to be declared a city.

When spring came the myriads of birds that found their way to the north was unreal. It seemed to me south countries were only stopping places to unload the weak and the weary. The rest all arrived up north. The foliage and the flowers were also quite sensational. One Saturday, Mr. Cook, the storekeeper took us fishing. As luck would have it, I caught a jackfish, a species to be abhorred by my husband of later years.

A certain airplane pilot would land at Thicket Portage from time to time to refuel enroute to Thompson Lake INCO Nickel Mines. He would make it a point to say Hello to us, and one day asked if I'd like an air ride. Up north we grabbed at any diversion. I saw a panoramic view of all the lakes and the river surround. It was quite awesome. I have totally forgotten his name.

When end of June came the north had gotten into my blood. I hated to leave, and I vowed I would return some day, but that day has not arrived to date. When I returned to Winnipeg the streets were so hot and dusty. I longed to be back in the north where the air was clear. I took the bus back to Steinbach and visited mother and siblings. Mother had expected me to have sent more money from my fabulous pay cheque of one hundred dollars a month with which I paid my share of groceries. We paid rent for the teacherage which was taken off our salary. I spent money on prizes for different contests I put on for the children. We also went to Teachers Convention, which required fees and a return train ride which the school board refused to pay because of some technicality. Paying train fare at Christmas and again at Easter took quite a chunk of money and again to get home.

It was very difficult for mother to survive without a pension. I don't really know how she paid for her medicine or for Lydia's.

THICKET PORTAGE

MY SCHOOL & TEACHERAGE

EDITH'S SCHOOL

DOGSLED RIDES

LET'S PLAY BALL

MY CLASS

class hiking day

PANORAMIC VIEWS OF SURROUNDING LA[N]

THE PILOT   WANT AN AIR RIDE, AGNES?

BOMBADIER/EDITH

AGNES & EDITH

TRUCK & BOMBADIER

BOMBADIER ON SKIIS   WAY TO GO

AGNES MRS. COOK EDITH

SCHOOL ACTIVITIES

CHRISTMA S CONCERT

JOSEPH ENJOYING LIBRARY PERIOD

MY CLASS AT RECESS

My 40 School Children

SNOWBALL FIGHT

FISHING & FRIENDS

LET'S GO FISHING

AGNES & EDITH

MRS. UNRAU & DELPHI

AGNES & DELPHI

FRIENDS- PEARSONS

LIFE IN THE NORTH

ROCKS ALONG THE RAILWAY WALK

40 BELOW

relaxing lake in back

**Mr. & Mrs. Cook
Storekeepers**

my feet in water?

NEW YEAR'S DAY 1955

KATHLEEN & ABE

SISTERS LYDIA, AGNES & KATHLEEN.

LYDIA, kATHLEEN & NEPHEW jIM

AGNES AT ORGAN

Spending holidays at home

CHAPTER VIII SUMMER SCHOOL AND TOLSTOI SCHOOL

"God made you one of a kind. There is nothing about you that surprises God. He knew your end before your beginning, your thoughts, desires, dreams, strengths, weaknesses, your failures, and successes. Nothing is hidden and yet God believes in you." (Peter Youngren)

I had always planned to train as a nurse and was accepted to work as Nurse's Aide in the Winnipeg Civic Hospitals. Two weeks in this hospital made me decide to take more Grade Twelve subjects and apply for Teachers' College. Many patients in this hospital had huge bed sores right to their bones, many having had infantile paralysis. I was personally appointed to a stroke victim. There was nothing I could do all day to make her happy or satisfied. I didn't comb her hair right, or I didn't lay her afghan across her knees properly, although I did exactly as she requested. Also, I was responsible for changing her diapers, an obnoxious, deplorable task which still retches my stomach whenever I think of it

Finally, I said to myself, "Give me children that are alive and laugh and play and have their entire lives ahead of them." So, I resigned and went to United College Summer School and took Grade Twelve European History by a good professor. Although I was not accepted for Teachers' College, I was granted another year of permit teaching because I had upgraded my Grade Twelve standing.

I don't remember who took me to the Tolstoi School, a town close to the United States border. Teaching thirty-eight students, Grades One to Eight, ten of them being in Grade One without previous Kindergarten, required hour long classes so I could get around to all grades. Again, my salary was one hundred dollars a month with an extra twenty-five dollars for doing my janitor work which included starting the wood burning heater for the school each morning.

Sometimes in the cold of forty below weather in wintertime, we all had to stand around the stove until the classroom warmed up enough for the students to comfortably sit in their seats. There was no such a thing as school closure for bad weather. The school door had to be opened for two hundred days each year and the teacher was expected to be there. The only time I had days off was when I broke out in a rash which was deemed German measles. I might have even been given a week of sick leave. They might have deducted the days from my salary, I don't recall.

I boarded in a Ukrainian home with a lady who was a terrific cook. Her goal seemed to be to fatten me up. I could not believe all the food she expected me to eat and she was genuinely upset if we didn't eat all the food, she set in front of us. I was always slim and a small eater, but with this landlady standing over me and compelling me to eat I did put on weight by summertime. She had a young boy boarding as well and she told me that she hated him because he wouldn't eat all her food. I think my thyroid started complaining after that.

To take over the Tolstoi School was a challenge to begin with. A local girl had also taught on permit the year before and wanted desperately to teach on permit again, especially in her home school. She could not understand why I could teach on permit a second year, but she could not. The chairman of the schoolboard eventually explained to her one morning at school that I had gone to summer school and therefore the Department of Education granted me a second permit. Finally, she withdrew and stopped showing up at the school every morning ready to go to work.

Next the students kept referring to this lady, Theresa as their teacher since at least one half of the students were related to her. One morning I had to explain in no uncertain terms, "I am your teacher this year and I will be here until end of June." After that the students settled down and knew I meant business. I appealed to them to be good so that if the inspector should walk in one day by surprise he would say, "My, your students are well behaved." A few months later that is exactly what happened.

I had to be totally organized every minute of the school day. Questions on the blackboard for Grades Seven and Eight. Workbook assignments for other grades. Hectograph copies for Grade One for Arithmetic for ten-minute sessions. Then on to Grade Two, then back to Grade One. We completed every Reader, every Mathematics Book, every Speller, every Workbook in every grade by end of May. One of the Grade Seven girls said, "Teacher, we have never finished our Readers before."

I had several challenged children. One nine-year-old girl had been in Grade One for three years. Her previous teachers had her sit at a table by herself and copy her Reader, supposing she was deaf. Her sister in Grade Seven asked me to speak to a certain lady at the Winnipeg Children's Hospital, which I did. She explained to me, "this girl is not deaf. She was very ill when she was five years old and she just shut it off. Try using flash cards." I told her I was already doing so. I also had her line up with the other Grade Ones to read a page when her turn came. I would mouth the words with her. One day in November she read out loud. Every child in the classroom listened. You could have heard the proverbial pin drop. Although at first her voice sounded quite guttural but by spring she was running around the school yard laughing and playing. I found this rewarding, more rewarding then all the average and brighter learners. I also put her in the Christmas concert in an acrostic that required exactly as many children as there were Grade One children. Her sister in Grade Seven said, "don't put her in. She will spoil the Christmas concert!"

"She will take part in the Christmas concert the same as the other Grade Ones. In fact, I need her to complete the acrostic." She had one line to learn: "C is for Christ Child who was born on that day." I think her sister really drilled her at home as she did her line perfectly.

I was always strict with discipline. On retrospect, I was perhaps too strict, but I could not tolerate having children walk all over me. Later at Teacher's College we were taught, "Start out strict, then you'll be able to relax a bit by November." It truly seemed to work like that. Bradley

School at Tolstoi was a two-room school. The principal taught Grades Nine to Twelve. At times I caught a ride home with him, other times I managed to get home somehow. I always set to work to help mother as much as possible by tidying up the house. Throughout the years I went home on Victoria Day weekend to make mother's garden.

On the last day of school, I said, "This is my last day here. I can't come back because I had a permit to teach here for only one year. So, I want to say good-bye and thank you all for being such good children." Then all the Grade Seven and Eight girls started to cry. It was always difficult to leave at the end of the school year.

Bradley School field day(Tolstoi)

THE PRINCIPAL?

SCHOOL MARM

WINNERS OF TROPHIES

ME.

KATHLEEN BUHR AND HENRY REMPEL WERE

UNITED IN HOLY MATRIMONY ON NOVEMBER 11,

1955 IN THE STEINBACH BERGTHALER CHURCH.

FOLLOWING THE WEDDING THEY MOVED TO

WINNIPEG WHERE HENRY HAD A JOB.

MORE EDUCATION & REIMERS'
DEPARTMENT STORE

When the school year was over, I still did not have enough Grade
Twelve credits to be accepted by Teachers' College. I took a job at
Reimers' Department Store in Steinbach, which was open from nine

in the morning until nine in the evening. I registered for some Grade Twelve subjects at the Steinbach Bible Academy. Fortunately, the store and the academy were only a few blocks apart.

I arranged with the store owners that several days a week I would work in the mornings, go to classes in the afternoons and work again in the evenings. Other days I would go to classes in the mornings and work afternoon and evenings according to the Academy's scheduling for the subjects I was taking. After deducting groceries, I took home for mother, the younger siblings and myself there were only a few dollars left at the end of each week. These I donated to whatever church I was attending at that time, possibly the Emmanuel Mission Church.

At home with mother and going to school were Henry, Lydia, and David. For me Algebra and Biology were always difficult. I have an idea I might have had to re-write each. Lydia took the bus to Winnipeg regularly to get blood transfusions. My heart ached for her for being so young and having to make her way alone. This happened before dialysis was in use. Doctors said the white corpuscles were tainting and devouring her red corpuscles and blood transfusions were the only medical solution at that time.

Working in that store was challenging to say the least. Two brothers and a sister were owner/operators. The lady partner had sustained brain injuries due to a serious motor accident. She often caused confusion with customers. For instance, if customers asked for bananas, she would offer them eggs or handkerchiefs. Her brothers tried to control her somewhat but mostly they apologized for her and let her do as she pleased. I just stayed on her good side.

A bigger problem: one of the brothers was an alcoholic and a much bigger hindrance. The rare times he was sober he was a good businessman, but those times were few and far between. His wife was a sister to our Uncle Ben, and we became friends.

Only one of the partners was stable and reliable. He taught me to be a cashier. He knew I was nervous during evening lineups. He'd put his hand on my shoulder and nsay, "Never mind the lineups. The only important person is the customer in front of the cash register. The others can wait." This advice stood me in good stead at Eaton's Bargain

Basement and other places of employment. This was long before scanning and automatic cash registers.

WINNIPEG JOBS AND FRIENDS

After that year I went to Winnipeg and took up a summer job with Moore's Taxi Accounting Office. In the fall a friend told me she was quitting at Dr. Mathers' and Dr. Stewart's Offices at the Medical Arts Clinic. I applied and was hired. Dr. Mathers was the first provincial psychiatrist of Manitoba. Dr. Stewart was a gynecologist. Both doctors were semi-retired. I was the receptionist, was in attendance with Dr. Stewart's gynecology patients to hand him forceps and other instruments and sterilize them through boiling. I also sent out statements and typed dictated letters. Dr. Mather's saw at the most three patients a day.

I took Grade Twelve subjects by night classes, Geometry and Algebra. I found an old diary where I read that I passed those classes that year. By the end of that year I was accepted for entrance at Manitoba Teachers' College in September 1959 after re-taking Biology in Summer School at the university. I remember we were dissecting frogs and I broke out in a fine, fiery rash all over my body. It was deemed that I was allergic to the formaldehyde solution used in the experiment, but I passed the class. Hoorah! At last.

That year while working at the Medical Arts Clinic in Winnipeg, my old diary tells me I had quite a circle of friends that seemingly just popped over any old time to chat and I also recorded many phone calls from friends. Our social life seemed to have revolved around roller skating, bowling, going to young people's meetings attending Grant Memorial Baptist Church, and so on.

Finding my diary now is quite amazing. I had been so lonely so much of my life but here seemingly I had a good circle of Christian friends. There were Margaret and Minnie Wiebe, Eileen Enns, Martha Kehler and her sisters, Anne Buehler, Jack and Frank Hyde, friends of Eileen and Martha, Gordon Senoff, friend of Minnie, Frank Remple and

Frank Funk's names came up in my diary. Frank Funk had taken me to Steinbach several times when my mother was in hospital there. He also helped me move from one suite to another with his truck. I recorded in my diary that Frank and another followed helped me move with a truck and I paid them each two dollars! What a lark! That would be an insult by today's standards. Was it then?

A few months later Martha and Eileen moved into a suite in the same building. We shared groceries and ate most meals together. My diary recorded how many times I took the bus home to Steinbach to see mother in hospital or to paint and paper the rooms at home or to do laundry at home for mother. I recorded that I had to work every second Saturday morning from 9:30 am to 1:30 pm. Sometimes, I recorded that I took the bus home on Saturdays after work, especially on long weekends.

DOUBLE DATING AT WINNIPEG BEACH

Relaxing ?

ANN, AGNES & CATALOGUES

I BOUGHT A CAR

EXCUSE ME. I"M GETTING DRESSED

CHAPER IX: WEDDINGS BELLS GALORE

Paul Buhr married Mathilda Friesen from Steinbach whom he had been dating for some time. They were married on June 27th, 1957 in the Evangelical Mennonite Church. They left for places west where Paul was employed with PFRA.

Lydia Buhr married Jake Friesen on October 11th, 1957 in the Emmanuel Mission Church. They later moved to Waskada, Manitoba where Jake had a restaurant business. The doctor warned that every child she would have would shorten her life by ten years but there was nothing he could do to stop it from happening.

David Buhr and Ann Schneider were married on June 6th, 1958 in St. Joseph Catholic Church in Winnipeg, Manitoba. They would live in Winnipeg where David had a job.

Edward Buhr married Sara (Sadie) Schultz from Swift Current, Saskatchewan on July 20th, 1958 in a double wedding ceremony with her younger sister and her fiancée.

Bernard Buhr married Helen Hiebert from Steinbach on November 15th, 1958 in one of the Steinbach churches. They would live in Steinbach where Ben had a business.

WEDDINGS

Jake & Lydia Friesen   Helen & Ben Buhr

Dave & Ann Buhr

Ed & Sadie dble wedding

Ed & Sadie Buhr

Honeymooners

Paul&Tillie Buhr

HOME SWEET HOME

WHERE THERE IS LOVE

"Nothing is impossible where there is love. There is no mountain that love cannot climb: No ocean that love cannot cross: No desert that love cannot survive: No winter that love cannot warm."

NIECES AND NEPHEWS

Sometime following the weddings, nieces and nephews started arriving. Those were very prolific years for mother's grandchildren.

John and Dorothy having married in 1939 had quite a head start and already had a family of eight children: Leonard, Ed, Anna, Peter, Susan, Dorothy, Ruth, Lydia, and Henry.

Bill and Eva had five children by now: James, June, Lawrence, Gary, and Wendy.

John and Rose had three daughters plus Marlene: Betty Marie, Mary Ann (Cookie), and Barbara Jean.

Kathleen and Henry had David and Dale.

Paul and Tillie had Bonnie and Penny.

David and Ann had Mary Magdalene (Mary Lee).

Ed and Sadie had Anita Joyce.

Lydia and Jake had Jayne Bethann.

I loved them all and was their babysitting aunty.

Nieces and Nephews

Back Row; John, Peter, Dorthoy

Front Row; Anna, Lenard, Ed, & Little
Dorothy

Kathleen, Henry, David and
Dale

Picnic with Dorothy's
Children and Aunts

Front L-R; Auntie Lydia with
little Dorothy, Auntie
Kathleen with little Anna,
Auntie Agnes with Peter
Dorothy and Baby

BILL & EVA'S CHILHDREN

JAMES & LAURIE JUNE

JAMES, JUNE & LAWRENCE

Mother

Lydia, Jake & Jayne

Jake & Baby Jayne

Ann David & Marylee

David & Marylee

Ed & Sadie & Baby Anita

Mother

AUNTY AGNES A FAVORITE BABY-SITTER

Aunty Agnes, nieces & Leonard

Agnes & Peter Gerbrandt

Betty Marie Aunty Agnes Barbara & Cookie

AGNES & MARLENE

CHAPTER X: GRADUATION FROM TEACHER'S COLLEGE

I lived in the same building as Eileen Enns, who came from Steinbach, Manitoba and Martha Koehler, whose home was in Lowe Farm, Manitoba. Gordon and Minnie, mutual friends of ours were dating. Gordon asked me if I would double date with them and a friend of his, a Christian High School teacher on staff where he was teaching. Nic Hyde was my date for the evening of June 17th. We went to a baseball game which I really enjoyed. Nic seemed surprised that I knew baseball rules so well, but I umped for my students' recess games and had familiarized myself with baseball rules..

We really seemed to hit it off and dated very steadily for three years. He talked about love and our future marriage at every date and he was onside with missionary work. We went everywhere together: to live outdoor theatres, to movies, to church services, to dinners, for long rides, for friendly coffees. He always remembered my birthdays and likewise I remembered his. We talked and visited for hours and he always declared his love for me. We enjoyed a wonderful Christian relationship.

I graduated from Manitoba Teacher's College in Winnipeg in June 1960. I was allowed to invite two people to the graduating exercises. I invited Nic and my brother, Henry, since they were both in the city, after which the three of us went out for supper to The Vineyard, a classy restaurant.

On retrospect, I should have invited mother, but then I would have had to find a ride for her from Steinbach and back. When I recently found her card of congratulations on graduating from Teacher's College, I felt that perhaps I had been remiss.

I did my practicum in a school in the city of Winnipeg and chose a particularly difficult group of children – gifted children. They require a totally different approach to teaching as I was to learn during the assessment of my critic lesson. I proudly displayed pictures of frogs and taught about the life history of a frog. That is not the right way to teach gifted children. We must give them a list of library books and tell them to find the pages that tell about the life history of a frog and then write their own stories. Regardless, I passed both the critic and the Teacher's College year.

That summer I had eye surgery to correct astigmatism on my left eye which I had since childhood. The doctor told me I would have a patch on only one eye but when I awoke from anesthetic, I had patches on both eyes. I was quite upset at first, thinking maybe he did surgery on both eyes! Fortunately, there was a simple explanation. According to my diary, Nic came to see me several times during my hospitalization.

GRADUATION FROM TEACHERS' COLLEGE

GRADUATION DAY MANITOBA TEACHERS'COLLEGE

GRADUATION PICTURES

AGNES & NIC

Agnes & Brother Henry

Me at my door on Spence St.

me on college steps

TEACHING CAREER

The Compass Of The Heart
By Jack Williams

You've sailed through troubled waters;
You've made it past the shoals.
You've kept the faith and stayed the course
As you've pursued your goals.

Without a star to steer by,
Without a map or chart;
You've reached your destination
With the compass of your heart.

GROSSE ISLE SCHOOL

I taught at Grosse Isle School the next year, starting September 1960, teaching Grades Five to Eight. Grosse Isle was a small town possibly twenty miles from Winnipeg and close to Headingly jail. The school board expected the teachers to live in their teacherage, but we were three lady teachers all living in Winnipeg and car -pooling to Grosse Isle. Rhonda taught Grades Nine to Twelve, Brenda taught Grades One to Four, and I taught Grades Five to Eight. I kept my small suite in Winnipeg

Again, I had a few challenged children. A boy in Grade Eight had never passed a Math test. I discovered quite soon that he did not know any of his tables, so I drilled and drilled with flash cards. Addition tables first, then subtraction, multiplication, and division. That June he passed with an 85 percent, an exam not set by me, but by another teacher in the district and also corrected by that teacher; which proves there was no favoritism. This area of his teaching had obviously fallen through the cracks. Another boy in Grade Six had never passed a Spelling test. Truly, his spelling was atrocious. Every week we studied twelve words by looking up meanings, writing sentences, copying the words many times until they could spell them from memory. The first week he had three words spelt correctly. He passed in June with sixty-five percent; not a terrific mark but much better than zero after many hours of drilling with word flash cards.

That summer I took a university class to make up one of the two classes I needed to make my teacher's certificate permanent. I had borrowed one thousand dollars from a Credit Union to pay my way through Manitoba's Teacher's College and I repaid it at the end of the year and still had money left over.

Nic and I dated throughout the summer. At the end of the summer, Nic invited me to join him, his dad, and his sister to go on a trip with them to B.C. for two weeks. I had already accepted a teaching position at Dugald, Manitoba due to start teaching. I had to ask the school board to give me the first two weeks off, which was very awkward for me because the first few days in a new school are important; meeting the new teacher and learning to know the children and establishing rapport and so on. I considered I might learn to know that part of his family better as I had already met some of his brothers. I was hoping this trip might help to move our wedding plans forward.

The opposite seemed to have happened. During the following six months, the relationship between Nic and me seemed to be on-again-off-again. Finally, I just gave up. We never talked to resolve our relationship. I was perturbed about a few things that would not ever seem to change – mainly interference by some of his family members and he didn't seem to be able to stop it and I wasn't aggressive enough to stand up to them. I could only foresee a future of calamity. They say it is better to love and to have lost than never to have loved. We had dated and loved each other passionately for three years. I was impulsive. That's who I am, and I often pay the consequences; "Don't cry because it's over but smile because it happened. What comes to mind was love and its power. If you have experienced it, I thought, it can never be taken away. When you have really known love, it doesn't matter if you lose it. That would be sad, of course, but at least you would know what it is."
Jon Katz

Many years later I met Nic in Regina, Saskatchewan where he was then employed with a government agency. The first thing he said was, "If I'd had my head screwed on straight, I would have done things different." If I could have looked into a crystal ball I might not have given up. Such is the pathos of live. We were now each married to someone else, both living in Saskatchewan. We visited over dinner but I never saw him again.

DUGALD SCHOOL

For some reason I can remember little about this school year or of the students. I do remember it being an emotional roller coaster about being on and off again with Nic. I believe that I taught conscientiously and well as before.

We Were three teachers all living in Winnipeg, fifteen miles distance from Dugald. Kathy taught Grades One to Four, I taught Grades Five to Eight, Jim taught grades Nine to Twelve. Again, the school board wanted us to live in their teacherage which was not happening. We all commuted. I had bought a car and passed my city driving test so often travelled solo. Sometimes I drove to Steinbach for the weekend to visit mother and Henry, then went back to Dugald the back way instead of coming from Winnipeg.

By now only Abe, Henry, and I were not married. Abe was employed with PFRA mostly in Saskatchewan. Mother was left with only Henry at home and he often came to Winnipeg looking for work but not settling into anything. Mother now lived almost alone. She had a wonderful neighbor who lived across the street from her. She was a retired nurse and gave Mother her daily diuretic needle which kept fluid from forming around her heart.

Mrs. Isaac told me at a chance meeting that she and my mother had been close. I asked mother to come and live with me in Winnipeg in my house, which I had rented at 93 Wellington Crescent, which of course included Henry who stayed with me whenever he came to Winnipeg.

"Remove falsehood and lies far from me; give me neither poverty nor riches." *(Provers 30:8)*

When I thought that my relationship with Nic was beyond repair, my colleague teacher at Dugald School, Kathy, and I decided to go roller skating one Saturday evening. After a while we both were paired off with fellows who kept skating with us time and again.

When the rink closed at eleven o'clock, we were offered a ride home by Kathy's skating friend. Gordon, in the back seat with me lost no time in getting my phone number, and from that moment on he was committed and supposedly smitten. He told me he was a trained United Church Minister and talked about how difficult his training time had been , that his family came from Wales and he wanted me to meet his family. When I did, his mother showed me a photograph album of when Gordon and his siblings were small. "Was that when you lived in Wales?" I asked. "No, we have never lived in Wales." A great big red flag waved at me. What else had he lied about?

He was constantly waiting for the United Church to give him a posting, meantime he was employed at a packing house part-time with his best friend, Gilbert, and he lived at the YMCA. When he asked me to marry him, a horrible fear gripped my heart. I told him I wanted to postpone any wedding plans until summertime. "It's just too rushed for me right now." We had mentioned Easter weekend at one time. With that he stomped out and left. I had no idea where he might be as he was not at the YMCA. The next morning, he arrived and sat down on a chair close to the door and he would not say a word. He would not come to the table for meals, but just sat there and sulked. Around four o'clock he left without saying a word or good-bye.

Surprisingly, his sister and family arrived on Easter weekend. .Gordon had told them we might be getting married this weekend When they heard it was off they decided to come anyways. I invited them to stay for tea. While I was in the kitchen making tea and coffee and preparing dainties she came and talked to me. Inadvertently without realizing she told me, "Gordon never trained to be a United Church minister. Is that what he told you?" In my fuzzy mind I had considered that I could do a trade-off with God and be a minister's wife instead of a missionary. But that was a lie too! She tried to defend her brother by saying that they had been poor when they were growing up and they had all invented brag stories which they all grew out of except Gordon.

Gordon's sister and family left and then he left without a word. The next morning there was a phone call from the YMCA that Gordon was leaving for the bus depot. I had pre-arranged and requested this call since he had my car keys and house keys and I was worried that he might take off without returning them. He was just walking in as Gilbert and I got to the Bus Depot. When I asked for my keys, he threw them on the floor and stomped off without saying goodbye. That was the last I ever saw or heard of him. Phew. I was glad I had listened to that voice in my conscience. I was so befuddled on the rebound from Nic that it took me a while to see all this.

FORGIVE YOUR FATHER

Mother read an article about mental illness and she became Dad's diagnostician. From that moment on, she appealed to us all, "Forgive your father. I have and so must you. He is ill and can't help what he does.

Forgive your father!" These words would ring in my ears for many years to come to come. Perhaps he was schizophrenic. As a child he would play with us, sometimes carry us piggy-back amid our laughters but with a snap of a finger he would become angry and abusive. "Forgive your father!"

DATING SERVICE

That summer I was very lonely. For so many years I had a steady companion to go out with, to go for coffee, to movies, to church, or whatever. Suddenly I had no one. I needed one more credit to make my teacher's certificate permanent. I enrolled in a summer course and mother had come to live with me. I joined a dating service as I found it difficult to meet men my age, even just to go out for coffee.

I had completed my requirements to Africa Inland Mission. I had spent seventeen years of my life focused on my goal, working, and studying and I never asked anyone for a penny. I had cleaned floors, washed dishes in a restaurant, I was an elevator operator at Eaton's department store, I was a cashier in Eaton's Bargain Basement, I worked in the Winnipeg Public Library. I had worked at Reimers' Department Store, I had worked for two doctors in the Medical Arts Clinic. I had taught on permit for two years.

I had never received any encouragement from family but was always considered the old maid in the family. Encouragements or compliments were rarely heard in our home. I think our parents didn't want us to become proud. But there was always an undercurrent of love, concern, and caring for each other, though unexpressed and in spite of sibling rivalries or occasional disagreements.

Throughout my life, I had to be totally independent in decision making. Now I had come to a crossroads.

THE CROSSROADS

"Take my hand. I don't know of anything in the whole wide world that's worse than being alone. Take my hand." (Elvis Presley)

I had reached a fork in the road. I knew I should now re-apply to Africa Inland Mission. Because I did not belong to any definite missionary- minded church, I would have to find a sponsor to support me on the mission field. This would be a difficult procedure, one which I had never considered before this. I would need to travel from church to church and beg for committed support. I would find this difficult.

Always in the back of my mind was mother's health and leaving her behind. Should she die could I make it back? I had connected with a widower dentist from Carlyle, Saskatchewan through the dating service. He had come to visit his sister and family who lived fairly close to where I lived and visited me also.

I had rented a house where I kept Mother, Henry and some renters. Dr. Wilbert Hewitt came to visit me in Winnipeg several times soon after meeting me. His wife had died of cancer, leaving him with two sons. He claimed he had not been sure he could love again, but for him it was love at first sight. I reasoned that if I went to Africa as a missionary I would live and die a spinster, and no one would care if I lived or died. I also wanted children; oh yes, I wanted children! My biological clock was ticking like crazy. Perhaps taking on two motherless boys would be a service in God's eyes akin to missionary service. It seems I was bartering.

I spent all these years totally focused on what I thought was my calling. What should I do now? I was now thirty-two years old and not getting any younger. My sister Lydia, whom we visited in Waskada, Manitoba knew she was dying. "Let us talk about death when you are dying. What else is there to talk about?"

She had asked me to care for her children, "and you can have my husband to boot." I knew she was serious though half-joking. I knew I could love her children like my own, but her husband? I wasn't sure. But I could always go back to teaching if necessary. When she became terminal in the Steinbach Hospital where she was born, I showed up to visit her with Wib. Her face changed. She thought she had a solution for her whole family. Why was life so crazy with choices now?

"Oh God of peace, hear now my voice,
In helplessness I cry.
And help me make the safest choice;
Lord, open Thou mine eyes."
(Albert Mombourqe)

LONG PLAINS SCHOOL

I had accepted another teaching position on a reservation at Long Plains School close to Portage la Prairie, Manitoba. Wib, as he was called, would come to my school, pick me up on Friday afternoons week after week, and take me to Winnipeg. At one time he brought his five-year old son, Cary with him. He and I got along amazingly well.

Wib was persistent. He made the trip from Carlyle to Long Plains School practically every weekend. There was no one else at that time who was there for me. At one time Wib invited me to come to Carlye, Saskatchewan. I took the bus to Whitewood, Saskatchewan on Thanksgiving weekend where he picked me up about fifty miles from Carlyle. When it came time to leave, he gave me his deceased wife's car to drive home with and to keep. Wow.

I finally said yes. We set our date for December 28th that year and I was going to give my notice to resign from teaching by end of November, one month in advance of the end of the school year.

THE SCARY NIGHT IN THE TEACHERAGE

One night as Anne and I were sitting around the kitchen table at the teacherage doing corrections we heard a weird noise on the roof, like someone was dragging things around up there. We listened and wondered what was going on. Just then I went to the bathroom and

I saw a pair of legs dangling at the window as though someone was letting himself down from the roof. I quickly closed the door and told Anne. We each grabbed a baseball bat and stood one at the front door and one at the back, making sure all doors and windows were locked. Anne stood at the back door in darkness and saw a large man whip past the door then on to the road.

When the police came next day, they did indeed see a pair of men's shoe tracks in the fresh soil beneath the window. They advised us to make sure all doors were locked as soon as school children were gone. A man on the reservation had been incarcerated for murder and had just been released and we were to call immediately if we heard or saw something unusual. That night I wrote to Wib,

"if you had come by on a white horse last night, I would have ridden with you."

CHAPTER XI: THE DEATH WATCH

I received a call from Mother one evening. Lydia's condition was terminal. The Steinbach Hospital staff wanted family with her around the clock. Would I come home and spell off the others? Edith Guenther, the principal's wife was the substitute teacher. She took over my classroom and I went home to Steinbach.

The death watch had already taken its toll on Mother. There were nights we each spent at the hospital all night. Sometimes we were spelled off and I lay on a leather couch in the hospital. I can't remember whose house our stopping off point was. We still had use of Abe's little house or did we spell off at Ben and Helen's house? John and Dorothy lived in Steinbach also.

The doctor kept saying she can't last another night, but she lived on. There was a suction machine beside her bed. Blood clots were forming in her throat and had to be suctioned to keep her from choking. She was lucid and speaking. At one point her feet were cold. A hot water bottle helped for a while. One evening she said, "My feet have had it." and she tossed the warmer. Later I read that when people are dying their feet are the first to go. Lydia must have realized.

Where were Jake and the kids? Who was billeting them? Jake was there almost night and day? Mother was with him one night when she heard Lydia begging Jake, "Promise me that you'll marry again." "WHY?" "BECAUSE you can't care for the children by yourself."

The evangelical churches were having special prayer meetings for Lydia's soul. At one point she had slipped into a coma and they prayed that she would come around so that they could ask her. Someone at the desk must have phoned. An evangelical pastor was right there when she roused and said, "Why did you bring me back?" Rev. Penner said, "we want to ask you if you are sure you are saved." She said, "yes I am." She then closed her eyes and went back into a coma. We had to continue suctioning her and be with her although she was in a coma.

One night around three in the morning mother was very, very tired. I took her to whatever house we were staying at., probably John and Doris.'; There was no one home there, but the door was unlocked. We had barely had a lay-down and covered with blankets when Abe and Henry came to tell us Lydia had just passed away, very peacefully by just breathing deeply a few times and she was gone. An angel came and took her to a better place with no more pain and sorrow for her. I knew mother would have liked to have been there but how could we possibly have known.? Hospital policy was that we could all go back and sit with her a spell. I don't remember who was all there.

"O Death where is thy sting, or grave thy victory? You are one who sends us on journeys and waits for us at the destination. When we find ourselves in valleys veiled in shadows, you are walking alongside us even though we may never notice.

Mother and I had paid a visit to the Loewen undertaker a few days previously. He was the one who had sold the house to Abe and said he had overcharged on the price of the house; therefore, he would charge less for the coffin and their services. We all tried to help Jake with the funeral expenses.

Lydia died on December 11th, 1962. Her funeral services were set for December 14th in the Emmanuel Mission Church in Steinbach. In the meantime, we went back to Winnipeg. We were preparing to go back to Steinbach for the services. John and Rose said they were bringing Dad to the funeral. It was a beautiful ceremony with solos, duets, a beautiful poem eulogy for a young mother, and service by the minister.

Wib came to the funeral. Dad rode with John and Rose, while most of us rode in the funeral car. It was such a sad situation for two little motherless children age two and three years old. They temporarily stayed with Kathleen and Henry. Over the years they had unhappy childhoods being shunted from pillar to post among Jake's relatives. They stayed with me for a few weeks soon after Lyle was born. Oh, why didn't I keep them then? I heard all their little stories of how they had been shunned by their cousins and aunts. How many times I have asked myself, "Should I have honored my dying sister's wishes, and mothered her children?" I know I would have loved them like my own, unconditionally. I could have always gone back to teaching if times were scarce. Am I making the right decision to marry Dr. Wilbert Harold Hewitt? Will I be able to fill a dead woman's shoes? Should I care for my dying sister's children and marry her husband? There was so much to consider. I should have had access to a counsellor.

After the funeral I had to go back to my school for another week. I had to pack up all my personal belongings and collect my salary for the month of December . Edith Guenther, the principal's wife was going to complete the school year with my students.

OUR PARENTS' PASSING

Working for God on earth does not pay much, but his retirement plan is out of this world.

Mother had two major wishes before she died. She wanted to outlive Lydia so that she could minister to her on her deathbed. Her second wish was to see me happily married before she died. She did get her two wishes in short order. She rallied amazingly as she had been ill previous to the death watch. She was probably in attendance with Lydia for several hours daily for a month or so before Lydia died on December 11th, 1962. She was in attendance at Wib and my wedding on January 12th, 1963 the very next month.

Mother died on January 28th, 1964 under anesthetic after surgery for a gangrened gall bladder. She had kept on living in my rooming house in Winnipeg, with her two sisters Aunt Eva and Aunt Gerty. Doctors were aware of her gall bladder attacks but because of her heart condition avoided surgery. When the gall bladder gangrened, they obviously felt they had no choice, but her heart condition did not tolerate the surgery. An angel took her by the hand to join with Lydia in a place where she would forget all her earthly sorrows. Perhaps it was Angel Lydia who took her away to a beautiful land on the faraway strand.

The night before she died mother had written on a note pad, "I have fought a good fight, I have finished my course, I have kept the faith. Henceforth there is laid up for me a crown of righteousness, which the Lord the righteous judge, shall give me on that day, and not to me only, but to all them also that love his appearance." (2 Timothy 4: 7-8.) My Aunt Eva told me that when the nurses found that notepad on her night table they wept. Aunt Eva also reported to me that mother had been in excruciating pain before surgery. I could well imagine having experienced ordinary gall bladder attacks. But a gangrened gall bladder must have been unbearably painful. As many times as people offered condolences I could only say, "she isn't suffering anymore".

Our son Lyle was born on January 21st, one week before his grandmother died. In fact, we were still in the hospital on the day she died. I called her from the Arcola Hospital pay phone on January 22nd to let her know that we had a little son, six pounds and twelve ounces. She asked if everything had gone well. I assured her that all was well. Little did I know that would be the last conversation with my Mother. Our son was ten days old when we travelled from Carlyle, Saskatchewan to Winnipeg, Manitoba for the memorial service. Mother had told me that she had bought a plot at Green Acres so that there would not need to be a collection for her. That's where the burial took place. Brother Henry had come to live with us in Carlyle and travelled with us to the memorial at Bethel Mission in Winnipeg, led by Reverend Uncle Abe Born, her brother-in-law.

Dad had deserted his family and found companionship elsewhere, but he did surface for mother's funeral. I never saw him again although he lived for ten more years. The other siblings reported his whereabouts from time to time. I understand that he moved back to the area of his birth in south-western Manitoba and married a widow with a large grown family. By all reports she was very stern and would not tolerate abuse. She told us tales at his funeral that he had converted before he died, which we all wanted to believe. He died of a massive stroke in May 1974. When I stood at his grave, I remembered mother's words,

"Forgive your father." At that moment I considered he did not know any better and believed he was disciplining, and I forgave him. May both parents rest in peace.

LYDIA

BABY LYDIA

LYDIA & FIDO

SCHOOL GIRL

Back Row L to Rt. LYDIA, JAKE, JOHN, MOM, ROSE, AGNES
Frt Row, BARB   Betty COOKIE. , ANN, DAVID

COUSIN REUNION

LYDIA STANDING BEHIND GRANDMA
GRANDMA HOLDING BABY JAYNE BETHANN

LYDIA & JAKE ENGAGED

JAYNE & JIM

DALE, JAYNE, DAVID, JIM

JAYNE AUNTY AGNES DALE

Jake & Baby Jayne

LYDIA'S LAST DAY OUT OF HOSPITAL

LYDIA, JAYNE, JIM, JAKE

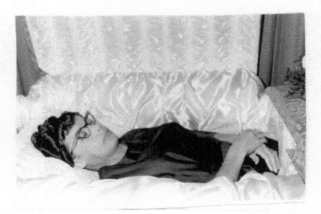

LYDIA'S SPIRIT HAS FLOWN WITH THE ANGELS

JAYNE & JIM

JAYNE GRADE 7, 1971

JIM

JAYNE

JAYNE GRADUATING?

FAST FORWARD

OUR WEDDING

DID MARRY WIB

We did have children

CHAPTER XII: WEDDING PREPARATIONS AND FAST FORWARD

We postponed our wedding date for one month after sister Lydia's passing until January 12th, 1963. During Christmas holidays Eileen Enns, Helen Dyck, and I got together to plan their gowns. Little Jayne Bethann Friesen, my little motherless niece was to be our flower girl. Aunt Eva was going to do the sewing. Wilbert's sons were to be attendants. Little five-year old, Cary Lynn was to be the ring-bearer and the older son, Glen Terry, and my brother, Henry James were to be the best men. My brother, Paul had volunteered to walk me down the aisle.

There were fifty guests in attendance, a small wedding by our choice. We were married in a little chapel of Young United Church in Winnipeg, Manitoba, by Rev. Rex Doan. It was a cold Saturday night on January 12th, 1963 at 7:00 pm. The reception was held in one of their small halls. Following the reception, the toast for the bride was given by brother-in-law, Henry Rempel. He used a popular slogan by Winnipeg bus companies at the time. "Agnes must think like Transit Tom – 'don't wait for spring. Do it now.'" A short program followed with my niece Ruth reading a poem called "God Bless You" and we then opened the gifts.

After the celebrations we left on our honeymoon, driving from Winnipeg to Florida. We spent a week or so touring, driving, dining, and staying at various hotels and motels that had vacancy signs. Then we started driving for home. The closer we came to this small town the greater my apprehensions. Were the boys, his sons, his siblings, his neighbors going to accept me? He was coming home to where he had lived most of his life. I was going to be surrounded by a world full of strangers. I had always been a survivor even by the nature of my birth and I would surely survive my new life in my husband's place of domain. I had to pinch myself to remind myself this is real. I am now stepping into a dead woman's shoes. My life as a stepmother and the second wife of a widower began, the sequel of which I may never write.

I was married to the widower dentist, Dr. W. H. Hewitt, and quickly became Mrs. Doc. I was quite amazed at how quickly I was accepted by most of the community. A few felt he should not have remarried so soon after his wife had died but we had to ignore those. To most of the people in the neighborhood I was somewhat a brave sensation, leaving my home in Winnipeg, Manitoba to move to small town Carlyle and taking on a ready-made family. My husband was called Doc on the streets and by everyone except his schoolmates where he grew up at Wordsworth, Saskatchewan from whom he got Wilbert, and his siblings and family called him Wib,, a nickname. Short for Wilbert.

We had two beautiful children together, Lyle and Joy, and I became stepmother to two sons, Glen Terry, age seventeen and Cary Lynn, age five. Amalgamating the two extended families was not a cakewalk, but my survival instincts kicked in. I must have done somethings right because Glen and Cary treat me very well.

We saw Jayne and Jim from time to time. When son, Lyle was two weeks old and right after Mother's funeral Jake brought them down to us in Carlyle. Why, oh why didn't I keep them then? All I remember was that my hormones were still working overtime from a difficult birth delivery. When Jayne was thirteen years old and Jim was twelve, they spent two weeks with us at our cottage. We also took them with us on a fishing trip to Niemben Lake in northern Saskatchewan, which they obviously enjoyed. I took them home via my green Gremlin SUV to Calgary, Alberta where Jake and his wife lived. We stayed with them for a few days. The cousins Jayne and Jim and Joy and Lyle got to know each other and had a great time together but that was the last time we saw Jayne and Jim. Circumstances and distances between us were all deterrents for us to get together. Joy and I did bring flowers to Jayne and her husband following Jake's death in Calgary many years later. May he rest in peace.

CONCLUSION

Birthdays are okay. The more you have the longer you live.

At this writing, I am eighty-five years old. Brothers Bill, John, Paul, Ben, David, and sisters Lydia and Dorothy, as wells as my husband and companion have all passed away. Why am I still here? I expect God isn't finished with me yet. He must have a job for me to do and I need to discover what more he expects me to do in the short time I have left. I felt that I needed to write my life story for my children and grandchildren. According to the law of averages and my genealogy there are definitely more years behind me than in front of me. I still have so much to see and to learn.

I'm thinking of the song, "Dear Younger Me" which asks:" If you could go back, knowing what you know now, what would you tell your younger self? "At some point in our lives some of us have thought if only we could do things over again. But the song illustrates we can't go back or change the consequences of our choices. All our experiences have shaped who we are.

My hope and prayer is that all my children, their spouses, my grandchildren, and their potential spouses and all who may read this may know salvation by grace through faith and that we may all meet again on that beautiful shore and be together forever.

May I be able to say as Mother did, "I have fought a good fight, I have finished my course, I have kept the faith" (2 Timothy 4:7)

APPENDIX

OUR PARENT'S STORY

Tena Braun and Peter Buhr's story.

Tena Braun, June 27th, 1899 – January 28th, 1964

Peter Buhr, May 31st, 1902 – May 1974

Married, December 12th, 1918

Our Father came from Gretna, our Mother from Letrelier, true.
They married on December 12th, 1918, soon after the terrible flu.
Into this union twelve children were born, though times so scarce they be.
Through war times and the Great Depression, they kept coming, one, two, three.
In the tapestry of life not only golden, pretty strands but also dark colors
Were woven into Mother's life even then. But she kept us all together
However difficult it be. Not one of us she'd part with, quote she.
Though fears at times beset us, we learnt to laugh and tease and joke.
Mother put on a strong front and taught us how to cope

My memories of Mother's singing and whistling come back to haunt me.
So often they were German hymns or sad songs like the mournful Lorelei.
That she taught us to love music we should really give her thanks.
By pinching money from cream cheques, she bought a gramophone,
The kind we had to crank. She slipped in some new recordings.
Some 33's and 78s. We all squatted on the floor to try to catch the words.
When all on paper were transcribed, we belted out the words,
Wilf Carter style.

"Hold fast to the right, hold fast to the right, wherever your footsteps may be,"
For this was Mother's prayer for us, you see.
My Father loved expensive Russian furs. That his children might not
have shoes to wear
Seemingly to him did not occur. His horses he did much prefer.
Our Father had a restless spirit and moved his family from place to place.
For many years they farmed near Plum Coulee, then to Saint Elizabeth.
From there to Hochstadt, then to Giroux and MacGregor too.
When things became too bad that no more she could face,
Mom and younger children were moved to Steinbach, hoping to find
some peace.

Our parents were not regular church attenders, but a young lass
named Nancy Koop
Started a Sunday School in the schoolhouse on Sunday afternoons at two.
Not once were we told that we must go but all with one accord
Dressed in our Sunday best and walked one mile to Hochstadt School.
The prize for perfect attendance was a Bible for which we all vied.
We learnt Old Testament stories, the Life of Christ,
Scripture memorization, hymns and choruses sublime.
And so, Christianity was planted into our hearts and minds.

All brothers eight have found fine wives, and sisters four good husbands.
All have lovely families though not without some troubles.
Whenever we all get together, we've actually grown into quite a large
Buhr tribal.
Some of our family are with us no more but have gone on before.
Sister Lydia died of a kidney disease as a very young mother in
December 1962.
Our one-week old little son his grandmother never knew because
Mother died upon surgery on January 28th, 1964. Father died of a
stroke in May 1974.
Brother Bill was called home in July 1997. All are waiting for us
now in heaven.

To keep us neatly clothed our Mother sewed fine seams
Oh, those matching seersucker dresses for sister Kathleen and me.
Fine foods she canned by the sealer full in order for our meals to provide.
Our Mother planted a garden, an acre each spring she would seed.
Or so it certainly seemed to us whenever she sent us to hoe and weed.
By the wheelbarrow full each fall the cabbages, carrots, and beets
were hauled.
But Mother planted a garden of far more greater worth.
An unknown author's lines I'll steal to end this nostalgic verse.

My Mother kept a garden, a garden of the heart.
She planted all the good things that gave our lives a start.
She turned us to the sunshine and encouraged us to dream,
Fostering and nurturing the seeds of self-esteem. And when the winds and rains
came,
She protected us enough – but not too much. She knew we'd have to stand up
strong and tough.
Her constant good example taught us right from wrong.
Markers for our pathway that will last a lifetime long.
We are our Mother's garden and we hope today she feels
The love reflected back from us

OUR MOTHER

Mom & her girls

Lydia, Kathleen ,Agnes ,Dorothy ,Mom

Agnes, Kathleen & Lydia

Four Generations

Grandma, Mom, Dorothy & Anna

Father in his Russian Fur

DAD AND EIGHT BROTHERS

I had eight brothers. When my Baby Brother Henry was born my oldest Brother Bill (William) was almost 24 years old.

My brothers in chronological order are: Bill, John, Ed, Paul, Ben, Abe, David, Henry.

Brothers Bill, John, Paul and Ben have passed away, mostly from heart disease except Paul who had several cancers.

Sequel: Brother David died of heart attack in August 2015

Henry, David, Abe, Ben, Paul, Ed, John, Bill, Dad

OUR FAMILY TREE

The family tree of Tina and Peter Buhr.

This is the geneology of my parents' children and grandchildren.

1. William (1919 to 1995) married Eva Friesen. They had six children:

Raymond James, Laura June, Garry, Lawrence, Wendy, Vernon.

2. Dorothy (1921 to 2004) married John Gerbrandt (1915 to 1996)

They had nine children:

Leonard, Ed, Anna, Peter, Dorothy, Susan, Ruth, Henry, David.

3. John (1923 to 2010) married Rose Coutu (died 1978) . They had three daughters and another daughter Rose had from her late husband:

Marlene; Betty, Maryann, Barbara.

4. Ed married Sadie Schultz (1927 to 1988)

They had two daughters:

Anita and Gloria.

5. Paul (1927 to 2005) married Matilda Friesen. They had five childrren:

Bonnie, Penny, Jackie, Charles, Jason.

6.(Ben) Bernard (1929 to 2003) married Helen Hiebert. They had three children:

Tom, Debbie, Ruth.

7. Agnes Neta married Dr. Wilbert Hewitt (1918 to 2005). They had two chilldren plus two sons from his deceased wife:

Lyle and Joy; Glen and Cary.

8. Kathleen married Henry Rempel. They had two children:

David and Dale.

9. Abe married Barb Doerksen. They had four children:

Valerie, Mark, Pam, Dennis.

10. David (1937 to 2015) married Ann Schneider (1940 to 2004).

They had three children: Marylee, Dean, Tina (1968 to 1983).

11. Lydia (1938 to 1962) married Jake Friesen (1925 to 2006). They had two children: Jayne and Jim.

12. Henry and Bernice Diagle cohabitated.. They had one daughter plus she had two daughters from a previous marriage:

Amelia; Taisha, Melinda.

OUR PARENTS

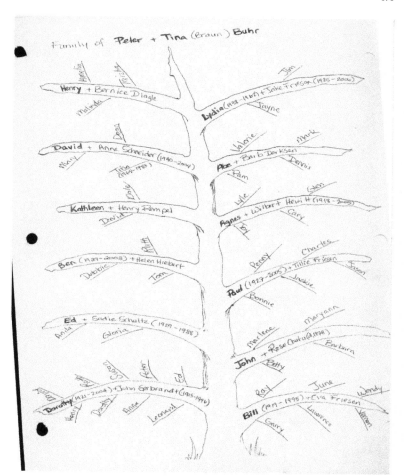

BUHR FAMILY REUNION MAY 2ND, 1993

SIBLINGS May 2nd, 1993   Missing brothers David & Henry
BACK row lt-rt. ABE, BEN, PAUL, ED, BILL, JOHN
FRONT ROW LT-RT- DOROTHY, AGNES, KATHLEEN